CITYSPOTS
AARH

C000230496

Patricia Smith
Paddockhaugh
Birnie
ELGIN, Moray
IV30 8SU
Tel: 01343 546860

WHAT'S IN YOUR GUIDEBOOK?

Independent authors Impartial up-to-date information from our travel experts who meticulously source local knowledge.

Experience Thomas Cook's 165 years in the travel industry and guidebook publishing enriches every word with expertise you can trust.

Travel know-how Contributions by thousands of staff around the globe, each one living and breathing travel.

Editors Travel-publishing professionals, pulling everything together to craft a perfect blend of words, pictures, maps and design.

You, the traveller We deliver a practical, no-nonsense approach to information, geared to how you really use it.

ABOUT THE AUTHOR

Based in Copenhagen, Nicol Foulkes arrived in Denmark a decade ago, fell in love with the people and their lifestyle and decided to stay. Nicol works as a freelance travel writer, teacher, language consultant and cultural coach. She has studied and worked in England, Spain, Germany and Australia and has travelled extensively worldwide.

CITYSPOTS
AARHUS

Nicol Foulkes

Thomas Cook

Written by Nicol Foulkes

Published by Thomas Cook Publishing
A division of Thomas Cook Tour Operations Limited
Company registration No: 1450464 England
The Thomas Cook Business Park, 9 Coningsby Road
Peterborough PE3 8SB, United Kingdom
Email: books@thomascook.com, Tel: +44 (0)1733 416477
www.thomascookpublishing.com

Produced by The Content Works Ltd
Aston Court, Kingsmead Business Park, Frederick Place
High Wycombe, Bucks HP11 1LA
www.thecontentworks.com

Series design based on an original concept by Studio 183 Limited

ISBN: 978-1-84157-922-1

First edition © 2008 Thomas Cook Publishing
Text © Thomas Cook Publishing
Maps © Thomas Cook Publishing/PCGraphics (UK) Limited
Transport map © Communicarta Limited

Series Editor: Kelly Anne Pipes
Production/DTP: Steven Collins

Printed and bound in Spain by GraphyCems

Cover photography (Aboulevarden) © Gräfenhain Günter/4Corners Images

CONTENTS

SYMBOLS KEY

The following symbols are used throughout this book:

ⓐ address ☏ telephone ⓦ website address ⓔ email
🕐 opening times ⓝ public transport connections ❶ important

The following symbols are used on the maps:

𝑖 information office		▪ points of interest
✈ airport		○ city
✚ hospital		○ large town
🛡 police station		○ small town
🚌 bus station		═ motorway
🚆 railway station		— main road
✝ cathedral		— minor road
❶ numbers denote featured		— railway
cafés & restaurants		

Hotels and restaurants are graded by approximate price as follows:
£ budget price ££ mid-range price £££ expensive

▶ *View of low-rise Aarhus with the cathedral spire*

Introduction

Aarhus, often referred to in Denmark as 'the City of Smiles', has a particularly open, friendly and positive vibe.

This is partially explained by the city's large student population: there are over 25 different academic institutions here (including a university), and, in fact, every fifth resident is engaged in some kind of academic pursuit. Their presence has created the sociological phenomenon with which, in typical Danish style, the city is identified – *den kreative grobund* (the breeding ground for creativity).

Way beyond the academic world, Aarhus attracts people who are generally open to life's possibilities, who want to initiate projects and actively engage with the city and its inhabitants.

This provides Aarhus's infectious energy and explains why it is so alive with cultural projects. For, in addition to the keen penchant for design and modern, urban development that you find all over Denmark, Aarhus distinguishes itself by nurturing a cultural scene that attracts and inspires locals and visitors alike.

Radiating out westwards from Denmark's largest shipping port, Aarhus is in the Jutland region. The city has youth – it's the country's youngest city – and good looks. It also has ambition: planners are transforming the harbour area and extending it northwards, in order to make room for new residents as well as to cater for the increasing numbers of tourists. A period of rapid, ambitious growth is underway and it includes such exciting ventures as the 20-year plan to create a *Sports Ramblas* – a boulevard exclusively dedicated to sporting activities.

🔺 *Cycling through the colourful city streets*

Other cities may be better known, but mere familiarity is in itself no recommendation; Aarhus has no laurels on which to rest, no tired old clichés to call upon and no received image to live up to. Few can match the city for beauty, friendliness and fun. Word's getting around, and pretty soon everyone will want a piece of the action.

No wonder Aarhus has a smile on its face.

When to go

Weather plus natural beauty make summer the best time to visit, and if you want to take advantage of the great cultural scene, come between May and October. During the Christmas period the city becomes particularly festive, with beautiful street decorations, markets in the Ridehuset and Den Gamle By and the smell of *gløgg* (mulled wine) wafting from the cafés in Vadestedet and the *Latin Kvarteret* (Latin Quarter).

SEASONS & CLIMATE
Aarhus's winters are considerably colder than the UK's, with the wind chill making it feel even nippier. The April-to-September temperature range is between 13 and 28°C (55–82°F), and can fluctuate between the two within 24 hours. Between mid-September and November, expect a reasonable amount of sunshine, but with some rain and temperatures anywhere between 5 and 15°C (41–59°F).

ANNUAL EVENTS
The city's gloriously rich cultural life is reflected in the number of different festivals and events that happen from May onwards. In addition to the most unique and popular event of the year, the Århus Festuge (Aarhus Festival, see page 16), there's a plethora of enticements at which this guide has room only to hint. Each year brings something new, so check what's on with the tourist office (see page 137) when you plan your visit.

● *Downtown has a bright festive sparkle at Christmas*

May

Colliers Classic Cykelløb (Colliers Classic Bike Race) Teams
from around the world saddle up and push off at the start of
the month. For further information contact the tourist office
🅐 Banegårdspladsen 20 🚍 87 13 50 10 🅦 www.visitaarhus.com
Vikingebymarked (Viking Town Market) Take this opportunity
to experience what it was like to shop at a Viking market.
🅐 Store Torv, Bispetorv 🚍 87 13 50 10 🅦 www.visitaarhus.dk
🅝 Train: Skolebakken; bus: 3, 7, 14 to Skolebakken

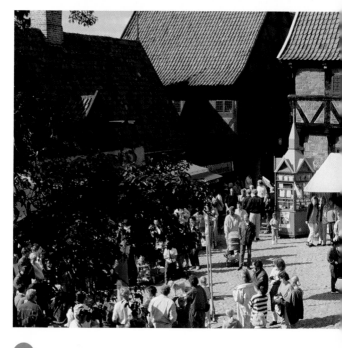

June–July

SPOT Festival The Musikhuset and Ridehuset become chock-a-block with Nordic rock. ☎ 86 12 84 44 🌐 www.spotfestival.dk 🚌 Bus: 3, 4, 14, 16, 17, 18, 25 to Ridehuset

Århus Middelalderfestival (Aarhus Middle Ages Festival) Midsummer (21 June) marks the start of a three-day re-creation of medieval life. 🅐 Vennelystparken, Nørreport ☎ 50 51 92 65

⊙ *Festival week in the Old Town has something for everyone*

🌐 www.aarhusmiddelalderfestival.dk 🕐 check website
🚌 Bus: 14, 56, 58 to Århus Sygehus

Sankt Hans Aften (Saint Hans Eve) The evening of 23 June
sees Århusianers lighting bonfires to celebrate midsummer.

Danmarks største chill-out (Denmark's biggest chill-out)
Grab a picnic and join the locals in the park for a late July
relaxathon, with DJs supplying trippy chill-out music.
🅐 Vennelyst Parken 🌐 www.stella-polaris.dk
🚌 Bus: 14, 56, 58 to Århus Sygehus

August–September

Sommerballet (Summer Ballet) Next, lug that hamper to the
Concert Hall lawn for ballet at the beginning of the month.
🅐 Thomas Jensens Allé ☎ 89 40 40 40 🌐 www.musikhusetaarhus.dk
🚌 Bus: 3, 4, 14, 16, 17, 18, 25 to Ridehuset

Pop Revo A three-day pop festival held in Pakhuset, a beautiful
warehouse by the docks (see page 77). 🅐 Nordhavnsgade 1
☎ 86 18 30 21 🌐 www.studenterhusaarhus.dk 🚌 Bus: 91
to Pakhuset

October

Mad-marked (Organic Food Market) This three-day event
allows you to experience Danish cuisine guilt-, pesticide-
and additive-free. 🅐 check website for location ☎ 22 33 14 94
🌐 www.organic.dk

Kulturnatten (Culture Night) A mid-month celebration of Aarhus's
cultural scene. 🅐 (Secretariat) Nordhavnsgade 1 ☎ 60 64 18 16
🌐 www.kulturnataarhus.dk

November & December

Juleparade (Christmas Parade) On 30 November Santa leads the Christmas Parade through the city centre, officially declaring Aarhus open for festivities.

Jul i Den Gamle By (Christmas in the Old Town) Christmas celebrations rage through December and end on New Year's Eve in the famous Den Gamle By Old Town (see page 64). ➌ Viborgvej 2 ❶ 86 12 31 88 ⓦ www.dengamleby.dk Ⓝ Bus: 3, 14, 15, 25 to Den Gamle By

---

PUBLIC HOLIDAYS

Nytårs dag (New Year's Day) 1 January

Skærtorsdag, Langfredag, 2 Påskedag (Maundy Thursday, Good Friday & Easter Monday) 20, 21 & 24 March 2008; 9, 10 & 13 April 2009

Stor Bededag (Common Prayer Day) fourth Friday after Good Friday

Kristi himmelfartsdag (Ascension Day) 22 May 2008; 11 June 2009

2 Pinsedag (Whit Monday) 12 June 2008; 1 June 2009

Grundlovsdag (Constitution Day) 5 June

Juleferie (Christmas) 24–6 December

Public transport runs to Sunday schedules, and banks, post offices, public buildings and most shops close on public holidays.

Århus Festuge

Århus Festuge (Aarhus Festival) has been taking place annually since 1965. Now recognised as one of northern Europe's most diverse cultural festivals, it encompasses hundreds of events and activities over ten days of dance, music, exhibitions, theatre, opera, kids' culture, sport and entertainment.

Unlike most other city festivals, Aarhus's pursues a specific theme each year. For example, 2007's was *I Bevægelse* (In Motion). (Others have included 'Womania' and the life and works of Hans Christian Andersen, and the next couple of years will cover 'Songwriters In Motion' and 'Århus Conversations'.) The fact that performances and events have to be relevant to the chosen theme keeps the festival fresh and vital. For example, 'In Motion' inspired the following kinetic phenomena: historical boat tours of the harbour; a children's bouncy castle in Rådhusparken (the Town Hall park); sports such as the Århus Festuge Cup table tennis championship; salsa workshops; Danish MCs locked in almost Viking-like combat at MC Fight Night, and much, much more. If it moved, it was in. This being Scandinavia, things always go a little deeper than one might expect: 'In Motion' prompted debates about the future of the city, the country and the world, the nature of time and – the big one – the movement of traffic through the city. It's like that every year. At Festuge, you can go party animal, arty animal or all-round Renaissance person animal.

Whatever the theme is, the whole of the city gets involved, and its parks, restaurants, theatres and museums all become specialist venues. The main aim is to have fun and discover

🔺 *Show spectacle, the Lions of Senegal, visit the Aarhus Festival*

the city's diverse and ever-evolving cultural scene, so if you're in town, you really shouldn't miss it. Actually, you won't be able to. ⓐ Administration: Officersbygningen, Vester Allé 3 ☎ 89 40 91 91 ⓦ www.aarhusfestuge.dk

History

The name Aarhus originates from the Middle Ages, but the location is referred to in Icelandic chronicles as 'Árós', meaning river mouth or river delta. The city's first real impression on recorded history is from the 9th century, when Jutland became the Vikings' headquarters. The trail then goes somewhat cold until the 1620s, when Aarhus was advanced upon by the Germans (you can still see some of their forts to the south of the city). This incursion seems to have woken various neighbours up to the good news that is Aarhus, and in the 1640s and 50s the Swedes attacked and occupied the city on several occasions.

What the Swedes and the Germans had realised is that Aarhus is located in a geographically favourable position: it is at the heart of Denmark on the mainland peninsular of Jutland, which meant successful trading with Germany, the Baltic countries, Norway, Holland, France and England.

In the early 19th century, the city really began to flourish and distinguish itself from the other major ports in nearby Copenhagen and Hamburg. The 20th century saw the city blossom, and its late development can be attributed to that period's Danish industrial revolution, when thousands of people moved from the countryside to the cities to find work. With the expansion of the rail network and harbour, the population increased to the extent that, by 1920, it surpassed that of nearby Aalborg, making it Jutland's largest, and Denmark's second-largest, city. Its most challenging period of that – and probably any other – century came between 1940 and 1945, when, like the rest of Denmark, it was occupied by the Germans.

Nowadays, the Inner City is home to just over 300,000 people. Plans are already laid for the expansion of the city to house a further 100,000 citizens before 2030. The University of Aarhus is progressing rapidly, with its academic record gaining increasing international recognition each year. The university, together with all the city's other educational establishments, places Aarhus way above the national average for educational attainment and contributes enormously to the city today. Another source of valuable cultural diversity is the 12 per cent of Aarhus's population that came from other shores. This unusually high number of immigrants (the national average is around six per cent) is made up of Lebanese, Turks, Somalis, Iraqis, Iranians, Vietnamese, Poles, Germans, Norwegians and Brits. Unlike, say, in Copenhagen, many of the larger migrant groups live on the outskirts of the city, which is just beginning to cause some tension as ghettos are formed.

The city is currently undergoing a major transformation, with the harbour area being extended northwards to create a separate social and living space, and various projects being undertaken to improve the integration of foreign nationals and immigrants. This is Denmark's greatest challenge at present; one gets the feeling that Aarhus's open and welcoming nature will see it through.

Lifestyle

In terms of lifestyle, the most influential word in the Danish language is *hygge* (pronounced 'who-ga'). A translation? That's a tough one – you'll only really get it when you've been here a while. But for now think of cosy, atmospheric, enjoyable and intimate combined and you won't be far off. 'Charismatic' might sum it up. However you translate it, the City of Smiles has *hygge* nailed. This is a buzzing yet laid-back place whose inhabitants operate at a distinct beat below the tempo of Europe's bigger cities. Perhaps most importantly from a visitor's point of view, Aarhus is quintessentially friendly.

Danes are spending more and more time socialising outside their homes: these days, workers frequently meet in bars after work for a quick drink before heading home (Århusianers are making an admirable stand against the trend for living life as a corporate wage-slave); students grab a six-pack and sit by the harbour, river or in one of the city's gardens. A definite café culture is beginning to develop. However, it is still very much the thing for locals to have a nice meal at home with friends over a good bottle of red wine and then head out into town. The manifold pleasures of social intercourse are of paramount importance here.

Take a leisurely stroll along the coastline beach

Culture

Aarhus is provincial (not always a pejorative term) in the sense that it really has only one centre (as paradoxical as it may sound, cities often, if you think about it, have several). But at the same time it has everything a big city has: cinemas and galleries, a mighty big art museum, cafés and clubs, great shopping opportunities and enough space for every expression of its inhabitants' personalities: there's a tango culture, a salsa culture, a street/punk/underground scene, a thriving gay scene.

Of course, it's not all unbridled hedonism: Aarhus has its spiritual side and might just as well be called 'Churches R Us'. The official state religion is the Evangelical Lutheran Church of Denmark, but there are also a significant number of Catholics and a growing number of Muslims. However, while most Danes belong to the church, very few actually practise religion and the country has a high number of atheists and agnostics. The church plays a cultural rather than a religious role in people's lives, as can be seen at Christmas time, baptisms, confirmations, weddings and funerals.

Aarhus also resonates to a distinctly academic vibe. The university has been growing constantly since 1928, making this a city of creative minds. Whereas its cultural life used to revolve around the academic institutes, recent cooperation between them, the city council and industry has been hugely successful: the cultural scene in Aarhus has exploded. The last quarter of a century has seen the advent of: Musikhuset (the Concert Hall, see page 72), which plays host to the Aarhus Symphony Orchestra, Den Jyske Opera (Jutland's Opera), **Det Jyske Musikkonservatorium**

🔺 *The Aarhus Symphony Orchestra performs in the Musikhuset*

(Jutland's Music Academy 🅰 Skovgaardsgade 2C ☎ 87 13 33 80
🅦 musik-kons.dk), and the Børneteatret Filuren (children's theatre
group); the Stenomuseet (the Steno Museum, see page 86);
and the ARoS Århus Kunstmuseem (Aarhus Art Museum),
the largest museum in Northern Europe (see page 68).

Aarhus is famed in Denmark for nurturing musical talent,
and the range of music festivals (see Annual events, page 10)
is evidence of its significance. Art also plays a great role. As well
as the larger galleries and art museums, be sure to visit some of
the smaller galleries and shops where you'll have the opportunity
to meet the artists themselves. Check out in particular:

Galleri Jarsbo @ Skolebakken 7 Ⓦ www.jarsbo.dk ☏ 86 21 12 86
🕐 12.00–18.00 Mon, Tues, Thur & Fri, 11.00–15.00 Sat,
13.00–16.00 Sun

Gallerie MøllerWitt @ Vestergade 56A ☏ 86 18 29 49
Ⓦ www.gmw.dk 🕐 11.30–17.00 Tues–Fri, 10.00–15.00 Sat,
closed Sun

Mogadishni AAR @ Katrinebjergvej 113 ☏ 32 54 25 35
Ⓦ www.mogadishni.com 🕐 11.00–16.00 Tues, Thur & Fri,
12.00–15.00 Sat, or by appointment

Ulrik Witts Hus @ Volden 23 ☏ 23 46 45 08 Ⓦ www.kunstruten.dk
🕐 10.00–15.30 Mon–Fri, 10.00–14.00 Sat, closed Sun

The inhabitants of the city are encouraged to get involved
in developing Aarhus's cultural scene. Strong Bright Hearts
(Ⓦ www.strongbrighthearts.com) is an internet community
whose members have started up projects like 'Share Your Heart'
(Ⓦ www.shareyourheart.com), an initiative encouraging people
to express optimism for the future. This unique approach to
development ties in with the general focus of the city towards
openness, inclusiveness and creativity.

⊙ *Summer crowds gather along the riverside in Vadestedet*

MAKING THE MOST OF
Aarhus

Shopping

Aarhus is made up of three main districts, Midtbyen (the Inner City), Trøjborg and Frederiksbjerg. Trøjborg's profile of somewhat prosaic purchasing possibilities means that tourists generally prefer the Inner City and Frederiksbjerg for shopping.

The major shopping muscles can be most pleasurably flexed in the Inner City. Three of its pedestrianised streets are known collectively as Strøget, and here you'll find Georg Jensen (see page 27), Denmark's most famous jewellery designer, fashion stores and all the usual high-street shops. The cathedral area is littered with shopping opportunities, including **Bang & Olufsen** (ⓐ Klostergrade 14 ❶ 86 12 29 22 ⓦ www.bang-olufsen.com). The Latin Quarter has numerous funky designer shops. For truly unique finds, hit the smaller, independent shops of Mejlegade, Klostergade, Badestuegade, Guldsmedgade and Volden.

The central station at the bottom of Strøget and the train lines mark the boundary to Frederiksbjerg with the dinky **Bruuns Galleri** shopping centre (ⓐ M P Bruuns Gade 25 ❶ 70 20 89 09 ⓦ www.bruunsgalleri.dk). Here are many international chain stores such as **H&M** (❶ 70 01 23 31), alongside sportswear shops, gift shops and the multiplex Cinemaxx (see page 35). M P Bruuns Gade is distinguished by a marvellous cheese shop, some lovely kids' boutiques and knick-knack shops. Wander down Jægersgårdsgade to find items for the home.

AND THE TOP THREE GIFT SHOPS ARE...

Georg Jensen Just the job for designer silverware. ⓐ Søndergade 1 ⓣ 86 12 01 00 ⓦ www.georgjensen.dk ⓛ 10.00–17.00 Mon–Thur, 10.00–19.00 Fri, 10.00–16.00 Sat

Hay A specialist in Danish design furniture and soft home furnishings and winner of the Danish Designer Prize 2007. ⓐ Rosenkrantzgade 24 ⓣ 99 42 44 20 ⓦ www.hay.dk ⓛ 10.00–17.00 Mon–Thur, 10.00–19.00 Fri, 10.00–15.00 Sat

LYNfabrikken The place to go for Århusian, contemporary designer gifts: lampshades, ceramics, jewellery, stationery and apparel. ⓐ Vestergade 49B ⓣ 87 30 00 75 ⓦ www.lynfabrikken.dk ⓛ 10.00–18.00

USEFUL SHOPPING PHRASES

What time does the shop open/close?
Hvornår åbner/lukker butikken?
Vohnor orbna/lorka boo-teeken?

How much is this? I'd like to buy it
Hvor meget koster det? Jeg vil gerne købe det
Vohr mah-eht kosta di? Yai vi gairneh hay di

This is too large/too small. Do you have any others?
Den er for stor/lille. Har du andre?
Dehn air fo store/lilla. Hah doo andera?

Eating & drinking

Aarhus's location – right by the sea, in the heart of an agricultural region – allows its restaurateurs to work with the finest produce that Denmark has to offer. Traditional eateries offering roast pork and potatoes, steak and some fish dishes are easy to find (Aarhus has Scandinavia's best fishmongers), as are more modern restaurants offering organic and vegetarian options. The city's large immigrant population is reflected in the wide range of cuisines here. As well as Italian, you'll find, among others, Argentinean, Greek, Turkish, Chinese, Thai and Spanish restaurants.

The Danes are a nation of wine lovers. Most of the cafés and restaurants offer a good selection of fine wines, many with organic options, but do be aware that the cost of the wine makes a big difference to your bill. Beers have also seen a revival over the past few years, with a huge increase in the numbers of reputable local breweries in the Greater Aarhus area and a broader selection of foreign and organic ales than ever before. Aarhus has its own signature beer, 'Århus sættet'.

Most cafés open between 09.00 and 10.00. Restaurants usually start serving evening meals around 17.00, and the kitchens

PRICE CATEGORIES
Based on the average price per head for a three-course dinner, excluding drinks. Lunch will usually be a little cheaper in each category.
£ up to 200kr **££** 200–350kr **£££** over 350kr

in both cafés and restaurants usually close at about 22.00. It is not customary to tip; however it is nice to do so if you have had a pleasant experience, 10–15 per cent being the norm.

The favourite everyday comestible here is *smørrebrød*, a traditional type of open sandwich consisting of a slice of dark ryebread with a topping. They are small enough to be a no-cutlery-required nibble if you're on the move or having a picnic.

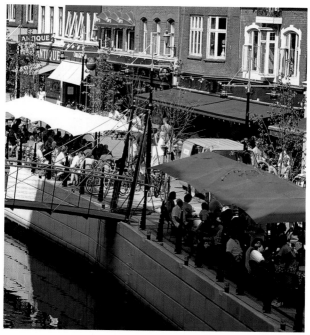

🔵 *Riverside cafés fill up in the Vadestedet area of the city*

PICNIC BASKET

There are several good delis, bakeries and supermarkets around if you want to create your own picnic basket or if you are self-catering.

Byens Ost A wonderful deli selling cheese, cured meats, snacks, seasoned oils, wines and more. **ⓐ** M P Bruuns Gade 54 **ⓣ** 86 12 24 74 **ⓛ** 10.00–17.30 Mon–Thur, 10.00–18.30 Fri, 10.00–13.30 Sat, closed Sun

Emmerys An Århusian bakery and small café which now has branches all over Denmark **ⓐ** Guldsmedgade 24–26/M P Bruuns Gades 49 **ⓣ** 86 13 04 00 **ⓦ** www.emmerys.dk **ⓛ** 07.00–10.00 Mon–Thur, 07.00–19.00 Fri, 07.00–16.00 Sat, 07.00–15.00 Sun

Gårdbutikken A small organic supermarket near the harbour. **ⓐ** Kystvejen 5 **ⓣ** 86 93 02 44 **ⓦ** www.gaardbutikken.dk **ⓛ** 10.00–18.00 Mon–Fri, 09.00–14.00 Sat, closed Sun

● *Emmerys has everything you need for your picnic in Aarhus*

USEFUL DINING PHRASES

I would like a table for ... people
Et bord til ..., tak
It boorr ti ..., tack

I am a vegetarian
Jeg er vegetar
Yai air veggehtar

Where is the toilet (restroom) please?
Hvor er toilettet, tak?
Vohr air toylehdeht, tahg?

May I have the bill, please?
Jeg vil gerne betale regningen?
Yai vi gairneh bitaileh rhiningehn?

Do you accept credit cards?
Tager I kreditkort?
Tah ee krehdeetkort?

Jeremys Bakery How many bakeries in Denmark are run by an English guy called – you guessed it – Jeremy? This one sells great bread sandwiches and muffins. ⓐ Mejlgade 17 ⓣ 86 76 19 13 ⓦ www.jeremysbroed.dk ⓛ 07.30–18.00 Mon–Fri, 07.30–15.00 Sat, closed Sun

Entertainment & nightlife

The nightlife in the city is mainly centred around the Århus Å (Aarhus river): the area along Åboulevard, known as Vadestedet, is the real focus of fun. Despite the number of students in the city, Aarhus does not really have a trendy club scene. The nightclubs that exist are actually discos, and men and women searching for that special soul mate are somewhat overrepresented. Still, if you fancy a bit of a dance among these strutting peacocks, try **La Belle Night Club** (❷ Mindegade 6 ❽ www.labelle.dk) or **Social Club** (❷ Klosterport 34 ❽ www.socialclub.dk).

Perhaps a more enjoyable (and certainly more Århusian) way to spend an evening is in one of the city's café-bars or even a *værtshus* or *bodega* (the Danes' version of a pub). There's no shortage of café options and seriously inebriated locals along Vadestedet; the Latin Quarter is slightly more peaceful, though. Don't miss the Teater Bodega (see page 76) by the cathedral and theatre, even if you just pop in to look at the amazing illustrated history of Aarhus's nightlife.

Another option is to go and listen to some live music. The venues are scattered around the city, but are all within walking distance of one another. Try one of the following: **Fatter Eskil** (ⓐ Skolegade 25 ⓦ www.fattereskil.dk); **Jazzbar Bent J** (ⓐ Nørrel Allé 66 ⓦ www.jazzbarbentj.dk); the Irish pub **Tir na nóg** (ⓐ Frederiksgade 40 ⓦ www.tirnanog.dk). Other concert venues

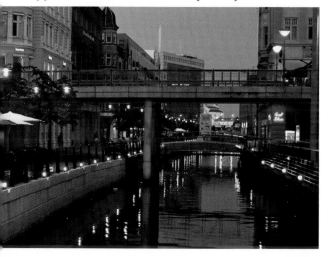

🔻 *Enjoy the riverside ambience at dusk in one of the many outdoor restaurants*

PUBS & VÆRTSHUSER

Aarhus is an old harbour town, and pubs and the traditional *værtshuser* are much frequented by the locals. Beers, shots and snacks are roughly a third of regular café prices, and many places sell a small selection of *smørrebrød* (the Danish open sandwich) and maybe some *frikadella med kartoffelsalat* (Danish meatballs with potato salad). Among the most convivial are:

The Cockney Pub Maren Smeds Gyde 8 86 19 45 77

Hunters Pub Frederiks Allé 97 86 13 63 50

Kurts Mor Fredens Torv 7 86 18 18 48 www.kurtsmor.dk

Peter Gift M P Bruuns Gade 28 86 12 01 63 www.petergift.dk

Sherlock Holmes Pub Frederiksgade 76 86 12 40 50 www.sherlock-holmes.dk

Strandborg Strandvejen 2 86 12 05 08

Værtshuset Nørre Allé 61 86 18 04 05

include **Turbinehallen** (Kalkværksvej 12 www.turbinehallen.dk); **Entré Scenen** (Grønnegade 93D www.entrescenen.dk); **Ridehuset** (Vester Allé 3 www.kulturhusaarhus.dk); NRGi Arena (see page 94).

Putative 007s should know that the city's only casino, **Royal Casino** (Stor Torv 4 www.royal-casino.dk), is located in the 5-star Hotel Royal (see page 40).

There are some excellent cinemas here. All films are shown in their original language and have Danish subtitles. Cartoons and animations often run in both English and Danish. The best are:

BioCity (off Strøget) ⓐ Skt Knuds Torv 15 ⓣ 70 13 12 11
ⓦ www.biobooking.dk ⓝ all routes to Banegårdspladsen

Cinemaxx ⓐ Bruuns Galleri, M P Bruuns Gade 25 ⓣ 70 12 01 01
ⓦ www.cinemaxx.dk ⓝ all routes to Banegårdspladsen

Metropol (in Trøjborg) ⓐ Tordenskjoldsgade 21 ⓣ 70 13 12 11
ⓦ www.biobooking.dk ⓝ Bus: 1 to Niels Juels Gade

Øst for Paradis (Art-house cinema in the Latin Quarter)
ⓐ Paradisgade 7–9 ⓣ 86 19 31 22 ⓦ www.pradisbio.dk
ⓝ Bus: 1, 6, 9, 11, 16 to Nørregade

🔺 Stop for a refreshing beer at the popular Peder Gift bar

Sport & relaxation

The sports culture in Aarhus is flourishing. The locals actively participate in a variety of activities, from tango dancing to handball and curling to bowling. There is no shortage of opportunities if you would like to get active while you're here.

SPECTATOR SPORTS

The NRGi Arena and NRGi Park are both found in Marselisborg Park in the south of the city (see page 95). The city's football team, AGF, and its successful handball team, Århus GF, have their home grounds here. Visit the website for a full listing of spectator events.

PARTICIPATION SPORTS

Dance is considered a participation sport here. The **Tango Akademiet** (**Tango Academy**) site lists the city's tango classes (ⓦ www.tangoakademiet.dk). **DGI Huset** motion centre offers all manner of tone- and muscle-building devices (ⓐ Værkmestergade 17 ⓣ 86 18 00 88 ⓦ www.dgi-huset.dk). For sculptors of the body beautiful, there are a couple of fitness centres: **Fitnessdk** (ⓐ Frederiksgade 25, Busgadehuset ⓣ 86 20 89 00) and **Equinox Fitness** (ⓐ Nørrebrogade 22–30 ⓣ 86 12 79 77 ⓦ www.equinox.dk). If you prefer to swim, the best pool is **Århus Svømmestadion** in Frederiksbjerg (ⓐ F Vestergaardsgade 3 ⓣ 86 12 86 44 ⓦ www.svommeanlag.dk). Just next door is the city's ice-skating rink **Århus Skøjtehal** (ⓐ Gøteborg Allé 9 ⓣ 86104219 ⓦ www.skojtehallen.dk. The only bowling alley is **Århus Bowlinghal** (ⓐ Eckersbergsgade 13–15 ⓣ 86 12 52 00 ⓦ www.aarhusbowlinghal.dk).

● *Ice skating in front of the Rådhus*

RELAXATION

Walking is probably the most relaxing thing you can do in
public in Aarhus, but if you prefer not to move at all, there
are also a few places in the city where you can treat yourself to
a facial or a foot massage. Try **Helle Thorup** (ⓐ Frederiksgade 33–35
ⓣ 86 18 39 00 ⓦ www.hellethrup.dk) or **Xenobia** (ⓐ Park Allé 5
ⓣ 86 12 03 10 30).

Accommodation

Most of the city's hotels are in the Inner City area, near all the major attractions. It's usually easy to find a room, and the tourist office, VisitAarhus Velkomstcenter, is most helpful (see page 137).

One interesting and unique alternative is the 'Kro'. These are usually found in villages outside town, so you'll need a car. Some are old, thatch-roofed farmhouses; others are country manor houses. Aarhus is surrounded by them – try Ⓦ www.krohotel.dk or Ⓦ www.weekendopholdet.dk

Camping is a good option if you're not perturbed by occasional changeability of the weather.

HOTELS

Cab Inn £ Located centrally and right on the river, Cab Inn offers affordable, clean accommodation. All rooms have a shower, toilet, TV and telephone. ⓐ Kannikegade 14 ⓣ 86 75 71 00 Ⓦ www.cabinn.dk Ⓝ Bus: 3 to Skolebakken; train to Skolebakken

Sportshotellet £ Located just 2 km (1.2 miles) outside the city centre in Frederiksbjerg, this is an ideal place to stay if you prefer

PRICE CATEGORIES
Based on the average cost of a double room in the high season.
£ up to 600kr   ££ 600–900kr   £££ 900–1,200kr
£££+ over 1,200kr

to be surrounded by nature. Clean, functional rooms.
ⓐ Stadion Allé 70 ❶ 89 38 60 00 ⓦ www.atletion.dk
Ⓝ Bus: 18, 19 to Århus Stadion

Havnehotellet ££ At the entrance to Marselisborg Pleasure
Harbour, this hotel has great views, huge rooms and
pleasant service. ⓐ Marselisborg Havnevej 20 ❶ 86 25 86 25
ⓦ www.havnehotellet.dk Ⓝ Bus: 6 to Chr. Flintenborgs Plads

Hotel Philip ££ Located on lively Åboulevard, the hotel is close
to all the main attractions. ⓐ Åboulevarden 28 ❶ 87 32 14 44
ⓦ www.hotelphilip.dk Ⓝ Bus: all routes to Banegårdspladsen

Hotel Guldsmeden ££–£££ A dinky, 100-per-cent-organic hotel
that captures the atmosphere of the city – warm, friendly,
familiar and homely. ⓐ Guldsmedgade 40 ❶ 86 13 45 50
ⓦ www.hotelguldsmeden.dk Ⓝ Bus: 6, 9, 11, 16 to Nørre Allé

Helnan Marselis Hotel £££ All rooms either have a sea or a forest
view. Located a mere 3 km (1.8 miles) outside of the city centre,
this is the perfect place to stay if you want to fully enjoy all that
the Aarhus area has to offer. ⓐ Strandvejen 25 ❶ 86 14 44 20
ⓦ www.marselis.dk Ⓝ Bus: 19 to Varna

Villa Provence £££ A super-slinky design hotel, with a warm,
inviting atmosphere. Rooms are spacious, and you'll find
it difficult to tear yourselves away. Perfect for romance.
ⓐ Fredens Torv 12 ❶ 86 18 24 00 ⓦ www.villaprovence.dk
Ⓝ Bus: 3, 7 to Havnegade

● *Villa Provence provides a romantic setting at night*

Hotel Royal £££+ Hotel Royal is the place to stay in the heart of the city if you want to splash out. ⓐ Stor Torv 4 ❶ 86 12 00 11 ⓦ www.hotelroyal.dk

Scandic Plaza Hotel £££+ The best features of this centrally-located chain hotel are the recreational facilities: there is a sauna, jacuzzi and well-equipped fitness room. ⓐ Banegårdspladsen 14 ❶ 87 32 01 00 ⓦ www.scandic-hotels.dk

HOSTELS & SLEEP-INS
City Sleep-In £ Here you can choose between a hammock in a dormitory or a private double room. There is a TV room, an info café with a wireless internet area, a basement café with a pool,

a small yard with a barbeque and a communal kitchen and dining area. ⓐ Havnegade 20 ⓣ 86 19 18 11 ⓦ www.citysleep-in.dk ⓝ Bus: 3, 7 to Havnegade

DANHOSTEL Århus Vandrehjem £–££ The reputable, well-run Danhostel is outside the city centre but has good transport connections. Choose from a dorm, a shared room or a private room. ⓐ Marienlundsvej 10 ⓣ 86 21 21 20 ⓦ www.aarhus-danhostel.dk ⓝ Bus: 1, 6, 9, 16, 56, 58 to Marienlund

KRO
Aarslev Kro ££ Good facilities, warm friendly serivice and a great kitchen serving rustic Danish cuisine. ⓐ Silkeborgvej 900, Brabrand ⓣ 86 26 05 77 ⓦ www.aarslevkro.dk ⓝ Local bus: 52, regional bus: 113 to Aarslev Kro

CAMPSITES
Århus Camping In the northern part of Greater Aarhus, this has two-, four- or six-person cabins, an area for tents, and a separate space for caravans. ⓐ Randersvej 400 ⓣ 86 23 11 33 ⓦ www.aarhuscamping.dk ⓛ all year round ⓝ Bus: 3, 117, 118

Blommehaven Camping Located just south of the city centre in Højbjerg, this wonderful campsite neighbours Marselisborg Forest and has its own beach. ⓐ Ørnerdevej 35, Højbjerg ⓣ 86 27 45 22 ⓦ www.camping-blommehaven.dk

For further hotel and accommodation listings try ⓦ www.visitaarhus.com ⓦ www.hotel.dk

THE BEST OF AARHUS

Whether you are on a weekend break or a more extended stay in Aarhus, the city offers a variety of sights and experiences that should not be missed.

TOP 10 ATTRACTIONS

- **Den Gamle By (Old Town)** Step back in time and visit reconstructions of some of Denmark's oldest buildings in the historic Old Town (see page 64)

- **ARoS Århus Kunstmuseum (Aarhus Art Museum)** An architectural wonder that's one of the biggest art galleries in Northern Europe (see page 68)

- **Latin Kvarteret** Stroll around the funky Latin Quarter, making sure you pause for coffee at **Altura Kaffe** (ⓐ Graven 22 ⓣ 86 20 28 55) or a beer at Ris Ras (see page 77)

- **Riis Skov (Riis Forest)** Take the bus, walk or bike along the waterside up to Riis Forest. A great place for a beach hike or a frolic in the sea (see page 83)

- **Tivoli Friheden (Tivoli Amusement Park)** Enjoy a fun day out with the kids at this small amusement park just south of Frederiksbjerg (see page 97)

- **Marselisborg Slot (Marselisborg Palace)** Visit Queen Margrethe's beautiful summer residence and gardens (see page 94)

- **Nordre Kirkegård (Northern Cemetery)** Who said cemeteries weren't groovy? This one offers stunning gardens and fantastic views over the harbour (see page 83)

- **Århus Festuge** Aarhus's annual cultural orgy (see page 16)

- *Smørrebrød* Savour the traditional Danish open sandwich (see page 29)

- **Fresh fish, organic veg** Be sure to have a mouth-watering meal at one of the many cafés or restaurants serving the most scrumptious local produce, such as Raadhuus Kaféen (see page 74)

🔽 *A row of brightly coloured Aarhus houses*

Suggested itineraries

HALF-DAY: AARHUS IN A HURRY
Stick to Århus Midtby – this is where most of the major attractions are. The buildings in front of the Musikhuset (see page 72) are architecturally impressive. Pop in to the ARoS Århus Kunstmuseum (see page 68), and pick up some gifts. The main shopping street, Strøget, leads you into the Latin Quarter where you can find several spots to have lunch or dinner and soak up the atmosphere.

1 DAY: TIME TO SEE A LITTLE MORE
Spend the morning in one of the museums found in Århus Midtby. After lunching in the Latin Quarter, either walk along the harbour or through Nordre Kirkegård (see page 83) up to Riis Skov. Alternatively head west out to Den Gamle By. In the

△ The tranquil setting of the old watermill at Den Gamle By

evening take a walk to lively Frederiksbjerg and treat yourself
to a gourmet meal at Malling & Schmidt (see page 100) or eat at
any one of the cafés or restaurants found on Jægergårdsgade.

2–3 DAYS: TIME TO SEE MUCH MORE

The best plan is to purchase a two-day Aarhus Passport
(see feature box below). Some of the museums, such
as Kvindemuseet (Women's Museum, see page 71) and
Vikingemuseet (Viking Museum, see page 70), are small, so
it's not unrealistic to consider visiting three in one day. Others,
such as ARoS and **Steno Museet** (ⓐ F Mollers Allé ❶ 89 42 39 75
ⓦ www.steenomuseet.dk), can easily take up half a day each.
Visit Marselisborg Slot (Marselisborg Palace, see page 94)
and take a walk around the surrounding parks and gardens.

LONGER: ENJOYING AARHUS TO THE FULL

If you're not pressed for time, make sure you take a trip out
of town to Ebeltoft or even spend a couple of days on Samsø.
Why not take a trip out to Bazar Vest (see page 48) and do
some high-octane shopping?

ÅRHUS PASSET (AARHUS PASSPORT)

This, the *sine qua non* of maximising your Århusian
pleasure, gives free admission to some of the city's
key attractions, free transport on the yellow city buses
(see page 51) and free parking at Skolebakken. See
ⓦ www.visitaarhus.com for details.

Something for nothing

One of the best places to go, where you really feel you get something of great value for free, is the Musikhuset (see page 72). This centre for performing arts is known for offering the greatest number of free events of all Aarhus's cultural institutions. There is no charge to wander around the building itself, which is a wonderfully bright space, perfect for freebie art exhibitions (which it frequently has, in the Balkon Galleri). The gratis performances usually take place at the weekend between 11.00 and 14.00. Århus Teater (see page 68) has also recently started to put on special free performances. Check websites or call for upcoming opportunities.

Aarhus believes that one way to ensure that art is accessible to all is to provide it for free, and many of its cultural projects benefit from state funding with just this purpose in mind. There are several galleries dotted around the city, particularly in the Latin Quarter, which do not charge entrance fees. This is a natural way to come into closer contact with the local creative minds. Many of the artists are themselves present and are happy to share their ideas with visitors and admirers of their work. As you wander around the city, look out for the omnipresent street art. Particular favourites in Aarhus are paint balloons: artists fill balloons with paint and hurl them at walls – there are a number of splatterings around as well as a lot of authorised graffiti.

● *An open-air concert near the Rådhus*

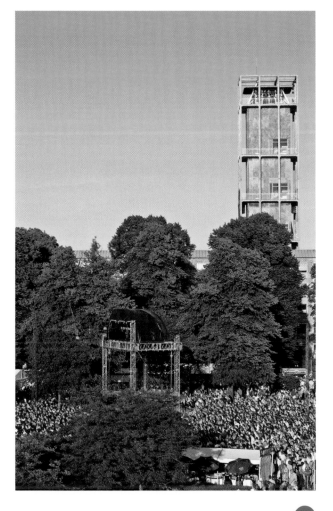

When it rains

Rain need not dampen your enthusiasm for Aarhus. If you don't have a car, the best option is to purchase a one- or two-day Aarhus Passport (see page 45). You can happily spend hours in AROS art museum (see page 68), which is a stone's throw from the Musikhuset (see page 72) and Rådhus (Town Hall, see page 64). Both are well worth visiting if you are interested in architecture and design.

If you like to shop and fancy a trip out of town, jump on the bus to the suburb Braband and head to the huge **Bazar Vest** (ⓐ Edwin Rahrs Vej 32 ❶ 86 25 42 11 Ⓦ www.bazarvest.dk ⓛ 10.00–18.00 Tues–Sun, closed Mon Ⓝ Bus: 5, 15, 18 to Bazar Vest). This fantastic covered market has over 70 different ethnic stalls selling all kinds of things: jewellery, food, clothes, soft furnishings, gift items and so on. There are also plenty of different types of restaurants and eateries; you will realise here how ethnically diverse Aarhus actually is.

If you prefer to stay in town, pop into either of the department stores Salling (see page 74) or **Magasin du Nord** (ⓐ Immervadz 2–8 ❶ 86 12 33 00 Ⓦ www.magasin.dk), which both have good cafés where you can enjoy lunch. Alternatively, head northwest, past the university to **Storcenter Nord** (ⓐ Finlandsgade 17 ❶ 87 39 42 20 Ⓦ www.storcenternord.dk ⓛ 10.00–18.00 Mon–Thur, 10.00–19.00 Fri, 09.30–16.00 Sat, closed Sun Ⓝ Bus: 7, 26 to Storcenter Nord), a large shopping centre just outside the city centre.

Aarhus is also the perfect city for café-hopping and people-watching. Start at Vadestedet, head up to Stor Torv and Lille Torv and round the day off in one of the many cafés in the Latin Quarter. Englen and Ris Ras are particularly fab.

If none of this takes your fancy, then maybe a rainy day is a good time to take part in one of the sporting or relaxation activities listed on pages 36–7.

● *Randers rainforest is a perfect place to visit on a rainy day*

On arrival

TIME DIFFERENCE
Denmark follows Central European Time (CET). Daylight saving applies; the clocks go forward one hour on the last Sunday in March and back an hour on the last Sunday in October.

ARRIVING
By air
Århus Lufthavn (Aarhus Airport ❷ Stabrandvej 24, 8560 Kolind ❶ 87 75 70 00 Ⓦ www.aar.dk) is located approximately 40 km (25 miles) north of the city centre. A 'Flybus' runs according to scheduled flights, making five stops, (Skæring Havvej, Egå Havvej,

---

IF YOU GET LOST, TRY …

Excuse me, do you speak English?
Undskyld, taler de engelsk?
Ornskewl, tala dee ehng-ehlsg?

How do I get to …?
Hvordan kommer jeg til …?
Vohdan komma yai ti …?

Can you show me on my map?
Kunne de vise mig det på kortet?
Kooneh dee veeseh mai di por korrdeht?

Hørgårdsvej, Tretommervej) outside the city centre and Universitetet (the university) in the city centre before reaching Århus Banegård (central station). The journey takes about 45 minutes, and tickets can be purchased on the bus.

By rail

Trains to Fredericia, Aalborg and Lindholm from Copenhagen central station (København H) all stop in Aarhus at the central station, **Århus H** (ⓐ Bangårdspladsen 1 ❶ 70 13 14 15 ❶ for times see InterCity or InterCityLyn timetables at ⓦ www.dsb.dk). The central station is easily accessible for disabled passengers, with lifts to all platforms and good toilet facilities. If you have any special requirements, call the station.

By road

The main bus station **Århus Rutebilstationen** (Århus rtb ⓐ Fredensgade ❶ 86 12 86 22 ⓦ www.bus-info.dk ❶ Bus and tourist information 07.00–22.00) is located next to the harbour. There are several operators that have routes to the Greater Aarhus area and further afield. These buses are all blue and are not particularly pram- or wheelchair-friendly. However, the local buses, which are yellow in colour and run by Midttrafik, are. There are also several X-buses that run express routes to other parts of Jutland.

There are a few main roads that head straight into the city of Aarhus. Nearest the coast in the north is Granåvej, which will bring you into the city along the harbour. Anticlockwise, the next major road is Randersvej, which will take you to Nørrebrogade through the university towards the harbour. Coming in from the

northwest, is Viborgvej, which takes you past Den Gamle By down to Vesterbrogade and Vester Allé. Coming in directly from the west is Silkeborgvej, which also takes you to Vesterbrogade. Finally, from the south west is Skanderborgvej, which leads on to Frederiks Allé taking you through the heart of the city.

By water

Århus Havn (Aarhus Harbour) is under development and may seem a touch basic. The Latin Quarter is located directly behind Skolebakken and Kystvejen, the main roads you are on when you leave the ferry.

FINDING YOUR FEET

As soon as you arrive in Aarhus you will feel a sense of familiarity. People are very friendly and used to foreigners; and you will struggle to find someone who doesn't speak English, so don't

🔻 *The roads curve around Aarhus Harbour*

be afraid to ask questions. The Danes are still resisting the euro, but kroner are very easy to get used to. Traffic is on the right-hand side of the road and there is bicycle traffic, which has its own lights (like mini regular traffic lights). Pedestrian lights use the usual red and green man; if you cross on a red man, you risk being fined. Crime is rare in the city centre, but keep an eye on your belongings at all times and do not take unnecessary risks.

ORIENTATION

The heart of Aarhus centres around the harbour and is well organised so the streets are very easy to navigate. There are two crucial landmarks: the steeple of the Domkirke (cathedral, see page 60) can be seen from the harbour, the Latin Quarter and the main shopping street, Strøget; and the tower on the Rådhus (Town Hall, see page 64) is clearly visible from Frederiksbjerg, Århus H train station and the lower end of Strøget. The cathedral is located at the top of the main shopping street (with the main train station at the bottom), right next to the theatre and several of the smaller museums, and the Rådhus is located with the station to one side and a large green area on the other, which has the Musikhuset (see page 72), ARoS art museum (see page 68) and other cultural institutes forming its boundaries. The district of Frederiksbjerg starts directly south of the main train station. To the north of the city centre, past the Latin Quarter (which begins after you pass the cathedral heading north) you will find the University of Aarhus and Nordre Kirkegård (Northern Cemetery, see page 83). On its northern side are the Trøjborg district and its main street, Tordenskjoldsgade. Running parallel to this street, just one block away on the eastern side, you find the lower end

A Communicarta
Style45® design
© Communicarta Ltd 2007 UDN.I
Map user Ref:WZFGICS/AAR/0724

1: Marienlund

6: Åkrogen
9: Lystrup Øst & Vest
16: Egå/Brohaven

8: Marienlund
56: Studstrup
58: Mejlby

7: Vejlby Nord

3: Trige & Århus Nord
11: Vejlby Vest
14 & 17: Skejby Sygehus
53: Mejlby

7: Charlottehøj
26: Skejby

4 & 24: Frydenlund

3: Hasle
14: Skjoldhøj
15: Brabrand N
25 & 55: Tilst

Skolebakken

Europaplads

6: Skåde /
Moesgård Museum

Rutebilstationen

19 56

1: Tranbjerg
18: Holme Syd

8: Dalgas Avenue

Busgaden

Hans Hartvig
Seedorffs Stræde

Rådhuspladsen

Banegårdspladsen /
Park Allé

Banegårdspladsen

Banegårdspladsen
(1 only)

Jægergårdsgade

Skt. Pauls Kirkeplads

C. F. Tietgens plads

Dalgas avenue,
Marselis boulevard

Tangkroken,
Dalgas avenue

1   18

Ingerslevs
plads

Lukas kirken

Stadion
allé

4: Skåde
24: Holme

Søgade

Baunes
plads

Hans Schourups
Gade

Musikhuset

Jægergårdsgade/
Frederiks allé

Frederiksbjerg torv

Harald Jensens plads

25: Søndervang
26: Nøddeengen
52: Fastrup
53: Ankersgade
55: Harlev
58: Langenæs

Rosengården

Silkeborgvej
Vestre Ringgade

Mølleparken
(Thorvaldsensgade)

Skovgårdsgade

P. Hiort-Lorenzens Vej

Søren Frichs Vej

Vestre
Ringgade

Lassøesgade

5: Hans Broges Bakker /
Toveshøj

5: Åby / Toveshøj

5: Stavtrup
9: Croftshøj
10: Mårslet
11: Osterby
15: Harlev
19: Moesgård Strand

5: Åby / Toveshøj
10: Åbyhøj N
16: Brabrand Vest
17: Brabrand Syd

of Riis Skov, which overlooks the bay and has Aarhus's closest beach to its right.

The Århus Å (Aarhus river) flows from the west directly through the centre of the city to the harbour. The top end of Strøget (the part called Clements Torv) actually forms a bridge over the newly opened riverside cafés on Åboulevard (River Boulevard) known as Vadestedet. You can get down to the cafés via stairs, or turn a left and left again at the cathedral, taking you along a street named Immervad.

GETTING AROUND

The easiest way to get around the centre of Aarhus is on foot, which is why we have listed some central locations without including public transport. However, for sights such as Marselisborg (see page 90), NRGi Park and Arena (see page 94) and Den Gamle By (see page 64), it is worth jumping on a bus. A detailed city map is available free from the tourist office (see page 137), the main bus station and the main train station.

All of the yellow city buses stop at the main train station, Århus H. Should you need a taxi, the best place to find one is the main train station at the bottom of Strøget: there are always plenty there.

CAR HIRE

There are a couple of car rental companies with offices in the city. Try **Europcar** (ⓐ Sønder Allé 35 ❶ 89 33 11 11) or **Avis** (ⓐ Jens Baggesens Vej 27 ❶ 86 16 10 99).

---

❶ *The old customs house*

Århus Midtby & the West

Neatly enclosed between the harbour and the ring road, Århus Midtby (the Inner City) is, like many areas of the city, easily tackled on foot (for locations where this is the case, this guide does not state public transport details). Art galleries, several museums, the theatre, the Musikhuset (Concert Hall), Rådhus, cathedral, the library, post office, bus station, main train station, are all located in this pocket of town, as is the very cool Latin Quarter. A longer walk or bus ride westwards takes you to the Botanical Gardens and one of Denmark's most unique tourist attractions, Den Gamle By (see page 64).

SIGHTS & ATTRACTIONS

Århus Domkirke (Aarhus Cathedral)

Construction started on this Gothic cathedral at the beginning of the 12th century. The building you see today was not completed until the beginning of the 16th century, and, at 93 m (305 ft) in length, it is the longest church in Denmark. It is also the church with the largest surface area of murals, many of which date back to the late 15th century (though one, painted around the so-called *spedalskhedsvindue* – leprosy window – in the northwest corner, dates from 1300). The interior is really quite stunning, and, if that were not enough, it has three organs. ⓐ Store Torv ⓣ 86 20 54 00 ⓦ www.aarhus-domkirke.dk ⓛ 09.30–16.00 Mon–Sat, May–Sept; 10.00–15.00 Mon–Sat, Oct–Apr ⓝ Bus: 3, 7, 14 to Skolebakken; train to Skolebakken

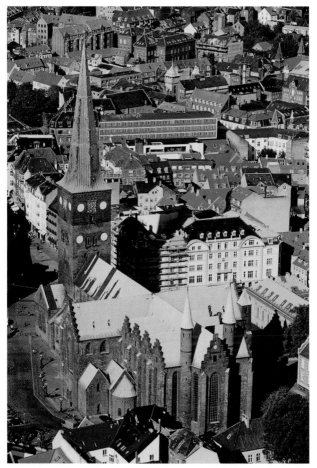

⬣ *Aarhus Cathedral and view of the Latin Quarter*

Botaniske Have

Den Gamle By

N

VESTERVANG

VESTRE RINGGADE

PETER HOLMS VEJ

LANGELANDSGADE

FALTHERGADE

TYNGGADE

SAMSØGADE

CROMEGADE

SANKT MARKUS KIRKEPLADS

DALLANDSGADE

SEJRØGADE

MARTIN VAHLS VEJ

EUGEN WARMINGS VEJ

JOHAN LANGES VEJ

LCE BOSTRUX VEJ

TAGE HANSENS GADE

VIBORGVEJ

MØLLEVEJEN

LANGELANDSGADE

NØRRE ALLÉ

MØNSGADE

GALTHOLMSGADE

SKERNVEJ

HENRIKVEJ

RINGGÅBINGVEJ

REGENBURGSGADE

REGENBURGS PLADS

SILKEBORGVEJ

DOLLERUPVEJ

DAUGBJERGVEJ

CERES ALLÉ

VESTERBROGADE

VESTERBRO TORV

VESTERGADE

MØLLESTIEN

GRØNNEGADE

VESTRE RINGGADE

J H SEIDLERS VEJ

A HERTZUMS VEJ

P HIORT LORENTZENS VEJ

Århus Å

CARL BLOCHS GADE

Bymuseet

THORVALDSENSGADE

LUNDBYESGADE

BISSENSGADE

FREDERICIAGADE

MARSTRANDSGADE

SKOVGAARDSGADE

Gods-banegård

AROS Århus Kunstmuseum

Musikhuset

MUSEUMSGADE

VESTER ALLÉ

BOULEVARDEN

Mølle Parken

Århus Kunstbygning

Kulturhuset

Ridehuset

Århus Rådhus

SØNDERALLÉ

GEBAUERSGADE

SONNESGADE

ECKERSBERGSGADE

CHR FABERS GADE

VALDEMARSGADE

SØGADE

BANEGÅRDSGADE

FREDERIKS ALLÉ

KRIEGERSVEJ

Århus Midtby & the West

0   250 metres

0   250 yards

Århus Rådhus (Town Hall)

This protected building, opened in 1941, was designed by the
renowned Danish architects, Arne Jacobsen and Erik Møller.
The famous furniture designer, Hans J Wegner, joined the duo in
designing the interior, furniture and other small details around
the building. What is most visibly impressive is its symmetry –
take a walk up the stairs to the fourth floor and look down. The
60 m- (197 ft-) tall tower, which was not part of the original plan,
was added at the request of the locals and has now become a
landmark. ⓐ Rådhuspladsen 2 ⓣ 89 40 20 00 ⓦ www.aarhus.dk
ⓛ 09.30–15.00 Mon–Fri, closed Sat & Sun ⓝ Bus: all routes to
Banegårdspladsen

Botaniske Have (Botanical Gardens)

Locals enjoy the charming Botaniske Have in Aarhus as a regular
park in which to sunbathe, read, walk, run and even sledge
when the snow comes. A stream runs through the park from
the northwest under the Chinese bridge and on to the dam at
Den Gamle By, where it goes underground and surfaces again
as the river, Århus Å. The tropical greenhouse is well worth a visit.
ⓐ Eugen Warmings Vej ⓣ 89 40 26 87 ⓦ www.aarhus.dk ⓛ Park
always open, greenhouse 13.00–15.00 Mon–Sat, 11.00–15.00 Sun
& public holidays ⓝ Bus: 3 towards Hasle, 14 towards Skjøldhøj,
25 towards Tilst

Den Gamle By (The Old Town)

Aarhus's number one tourist attraction. This wonderful,
reconstructed Old Town breathes the history of Aarhus over the
past 400 years, with everyone in traditional dress pretending

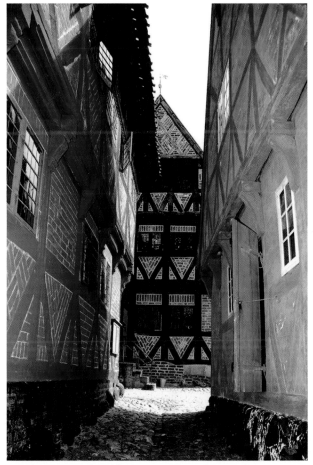

⌃ *Detail of traditional houses in the open-air museum of Den Gamle By*

to carry out the daily tasks of residents of an old Danish town from the late 1500s to the 1920s. The town hosts the **Dansk Plakat Museum (Danish Poster Museum** ⓐ Ludvig Feilbergsveg 7 ⓘ 86 15 33 45 ⓦ plakatmuseum.dk), **Det Danske Urmuseum (The Danish Clock Museum)** and has a big **Lejetøjsmuseum (Toy Museum)**. Visit the tractor sheds, the local grocery store, the baker, the book shop, the ironmonger and many other shops and places of work. There is an abundance of activities for children to take part in and a rather tempting sweet shop where they can help make the confectionery. This is a great place to visit at Christmas. Between Easter and Christmas it is high season and

⬥ *Quaint Møllestien is a peaceful haven in the city*

there are always special events and exhibitions, particularly during Århus Festuge. ⓐ Viborgvej 2 ⓣ 86 12 31 88 ⓦ www.dengamleby.dk ⓝ Bus: 3, 14, 25 to Den Gamle By. Admission charge

Møllestien (Mill Lane)

Møllestien is known as the most beautiful street in Aarhus. Most of its houses date back to the 18th century; the colourful façades, cobbled road and pretty flowers in hanging baskets give you the feeling of being in a small Danish village. Archaeological excavations revealed pottery dating back as far as the Middle Ages outside number 53, where – surprise, surprise – you can now buy classical Danish pottery items.

CULTURE

Århus Kunstbygning (Aarhus Centre for Contemporary Art)

This original, wonderful exhibition space was completed at the beginning of the 20th century. The aim of the Kunstbygning (which translates as 'art building') is to house a whole range of artistic expression from painting, sculpture and photography to performance, film and video. There are different exhibitions more or less every two months, and the venue is popular among up-and-coming Århusian creative talents. There are also often classical, jazz, rhythmic and electronic music concerts held here. ⓐ J M Mørks Gade 13 ⓣ 86 20 60 50 ⓦ www.aarhuskynstbygning.dk ⓛ 10.00–17.00 Tues & Thur–Sun, 10.00–21.00 Wed, closed Mon ⓝ Bus: 5, 6, 7, 9, 10, 11 to Østergade ❶ Guided tours in English upon request

Århus Teater (Aarhus Theatre)

Even if you don't see a performance, you shouldn't miss this beautiful protected building from 1900. With pretty, flowered, stained-glass windows and flora and fauna designs on the arched ceilings, it was designed by Hack Kampmann, the brains behind several prominent buildings in Aarhus, including Queen Margrethe's summer residence, Marselisborg Slot (see page 94). The swan ceiling in the main auditorium is a sight to behold. Tours of the theatre are held for the public on the first Saturday of the month during the theatre season (September to December). ⓐ Teatergaden ⓣ 89 33 23 00 ⓦ www.aarhusteater.dk ⓛ doors open half an hour before the start of the performance ⓝ Bus: 3, 7, 14 to Skolebakken; train to Skolebakken. Admission charge, Mon half-price

ARoS Århus Kunstmuseum (Aarhus Art Museum)

Big is meaningful at this international art museum, which opened in 2004. Its 17,700 sq m (58,000 sq ft) are divided up over nine floors, making one of Northern Europe's largest museums. There are three galleries with permanent exhibitions displaying art from 1770 up to the present day, and a gallery on the ground floor specially designed for light and video installations. As well as housing the world's largest Per Kirkeby collection, ARoS features international artists such as James Turrell, Miwa Yanagi and Gilbert & George. There is also a fantastic junior museum with a workshop for the kids, a novel gift-shop right at the entrance, **ART Restaurant** on the eighth floor (ⓛ 10.00–17.00 Tues & Thur–Sun, 10.00–22.00 Wed), and **ART Café** on the ground floor (ⓛ 10.00–16.45 Tues & Thur–Sun, 10.00–21.45 Wed). ⓐ Aros Allé 2 ⓣ 87 30 66 00 ⓦ www.aros.dk

● *The wonderful winding staircase at ARoS*

🕙 10.00–17.00 Tues & Thur–Sun, 10.00–22.00 Wed, closed Mon
🚌 Bus: 3, 4, 14, 16, 17, 18, 25 to Ridehuset. Admission charge,
under 18s free

Besættelsesmuseet (The Occupation Museum)

A suitably dignified museum that tells the history of Aarhus during
the German occupation between 1940 and 1945. Artefacts from the
Nazi and Danish military, propaganda, documents, posters and
other memorabilia from that time are displayed in the former town
hall and police station. 📍 Mathilde Fibigers Have 2 📞 86 18 42 77
🌐 www.besaettelsesmuseet.dk 🕙 11.00–16.00 Sat & Sun, Jan & Dec;
11.00–16.00 Tues, Thur, Sat & Sun, June–Aug 🚌 Bus: 3, 7 to Skolebakken;
train to Skolebakken. Admission charge, under 18s free

VIKINGEMUSEET (VIKING MUSEUM)

It's good to be reminded that, despite what it says in the
films, Vikings weren't just a bunch of pillagers, plunderers
and practitioners of non-consensual sex. This tiny, unique
museum, located in the basement under Nordea Bank,
gives a comprehensive history of the city when it was still
called "Aros" and, in doing so, reveals that the Vikings were
organised administrators, skilled craftspeople and expert
navigators. Several of the pieces displayed here were
excavated at this precise location. 📍 St Clemens Torv 6
📞 Moesgård Museum 89 42 11 00 🌐 www.vikingemuseet.dk
🕙 10.00–16.00 Mon, Tues, Wed & Fri, 10.00–17.30 Thur, closed
Sat & Sun 🚌 Bus: 3, 7,14 to Skolebakken; train to Skolebakken

Bymuseet (The Town Museum)

The Bymuseet is the ideal place to get a comprehensive overview of the history of the Greater Aarhus region since post-Viking days. The building itself is of historical and architectural significance, with the original part being the old Hammel station house. A new part of the building was designed to maximise the green area situated at the rear. An interesting and striking combination of panes of glass and wood panelling create the other face of Bymuseet. ⓐ Carl Blochs Gade 28 ⓣ 86 13 28 62 ⓦ www.bymuseet.dk ⓛ 10.00–17.00 Thur–Tues, 10.00–20.00 Wed ⓝ Bus: 18 to Skovgårdsgade. Admission charge, under 18s free

Kulturhuset (The Culture House)

The aim of Kulturhuset is to give local artists a professional environment in which to work. The building houses advisors, teachers, workshops and studios. Ridehuset, which is run by Kulturhuset, is currently used to house *loppemarkeder* (flea markets), concerts, theatre productions, trade fairs and so on, and is therefore considered an important venue in Aarhus's cultural life. It is the perfect location for some of Aarhus's major cultural events (see Annual events, page 10). **Brobjergskolen** (ⓐ Frederiks Allé 20) is also part of the Culture House and is home to one of the city's dance schools. ⓐ Vester Allé 3 ⓣ 89 40 23 90 ⓦ www.kulturhusaarhus.dk ⓝ Bus: 3, 4, 14, 16, 17, 18, 25 to Ridehuset

Kvindemuseet (The Women's Museum)

It should come as no surprise that the country with a solid reputation for gender equality has its own Women's Museum. This wonderful, tiny institution pays homage to the female of the species by covering themes of childbirth, work, education and daily life. With small displays it presents a history of women from prehistoric times to the present day and features prominent Danish women who played a significant role in the feminist movement of the 1970s. There is also the very popular Barndommens Museum (Childhood Museum) here, and the cosy little café is well worth a visit.

⬥ *Childbirth on display at the Kvindemuseet*

🅐 Domkirkeplads 5 ☎ 86 18 64 70 🅦 www.womensmuseum.dk
🕒 10.00–17.00 Mon, Tues & Thur, 10.00–20.00 Wed, 11.00–17.00 Sat & Sun, June–Aug; 10.00–16.00 Tues, Thur & Fri, 10.00–20.00 Wed, closed Mon, Sept–May 🅝 Bus: 3, 7 to Skolebakken; train to Skolebakken. Admission charge, under 18s free

Musikhuset (The Concert Hall)

The stats say it all: this cultural institute attracts over half a million visitors every year. It brings together three of the city's major performing arts groups: the Aarhus Symphony Orchestra performs in the Symfonisk Sal; Filuren (the children's theatre group) runs a school for kids and puts on performances for both adults and children; Det Jyske Musikkonservatorium's (The Jutland Academy of Music, see page 22) 290 students and 70 staff are gathered in the Rytmisk Sal. Famous names such as Liza Minelli, Tina Turner and Sting have all performed here. Musikhuset is open to the public, whether there are performances on or not, and often has free art exhibitions on the balcony. Just wander around and admire the wonderful bright spaces, comparing the old glass building from the 1980s with the modern extension behind the ticket office (notice the small room above the ticket office where Queen Margrethe sits during the intermission), or grab a bite to eat at one of the three restaurants. The gardens in front of the Concert Hall, known as Musikhusets Parken, are also quite special, having been designed to be enjoyed and navigated by all, particularly the disabled, blind and deaf. Different features such as paving stones, water features and aromatic flora and fauna are dotted around. ⓐ Thomas Jensens Allé ⓣ 89 40 40 40 ⓦ www.musikhusetaarhus.dk ⓒ Foyer & tickets 10.00–18.00 June–Aug; 10.00–21.00 Sept–May, Entrance to the stage 06.45–18.00 Mon–Fri, 09.30–18.00 Sat & Sun, June–Aug; 06.45–21.00 Sept–May ⓝ Bus: 3, 4, 14, 16, 17, 18, 25 to Ridehuset

RETAIL THERAPY

Box de Lux Specialising in stylish storage, this delightful boutique sells all sorts of boxes and knick-knacks for the home. A great place to find small designer gifts. ⓐ Graven 24 ⓣ 86 12 60 04 ⓦ www.boxdelux.dk ⓒ 10.00–17.30 Mon–Thur, 10.00–19.00 Fri, 10.00–14.00 Sat, closed Sun

Junk de Luxe Great Århusian designer clothes shop, particularly for men, with customised second-hand clothing. ⓐ Studsgade 2–4

☎ 86 12 90 00 **ⓦ** www.junkdeluxe.dk **🕐** 11.00–18.00 Mon–Thur, 11.00–19.00 Fri, 10.00–15.00 Sat, closed Sun

Salling A pleasant department store famed for its high quality standards and good atmosphere. As well as a great supermarket, Salling Super, in the basement, the store houses over 35 retailers selling clothing, shoes, perfume, books, toys and household wares. **ⓐ** Søndergade 27 **☎** 86 12 18 00 **ⓦ** www.salling.dk **🕐** 09.30–18.30 Mon–Wed, 09.30–20.00 Thur & Fri, 09.00–17.00 Sat

TAKING A BREAK

Raadhuus Kaféen £ **❶** Everything here is traditionally Danish. Lots of meat and fish, but not much for vegetarians. **ⓐ** Sønder Allé 3 **☎** 86 12 37 74 **ⓦ** www.raadhuus-kafeen.dk **🕐** 11.00–23.00 Mon–Sat, 12.00–22.00 Sun, kitchen closes one hour earlier

Sigfreds Kaffebar £ **❷** Great little coffee bar and snackerie. Drink in or take-away at either of the two bars in Ryesgade. At number 3 the coffee bar is located in the wonderful Vangsgaards bookshop – very relaxing atmosphere. **ⓐ** Ryesgade 28 & Ryesgade 3 **☎** 86 18 08 19/86 18 08 16 **ⓦ** www.sigfreds-kaffebar.dk **🕐** (number 28) 08.30–18.30 Mon–Thur, 08.30–20.00 Fri, 09.30–18.00 Sat, closed Sun; (number 3) 10.00–17.30 Mon–Thur, 10.00–19.00 Fri, 10.00–16.00 Sat, closed Sun

🔺 *Café Englen is warm and inviting*

Café Englen £–££ ❸ French-brasserie-style café that's a gem
of the Latin Quarter, with its warm interior and relaxing
courtyard area. Serves organic beverages and a limited but
delicious lunch and dinner menu. ❹ Studsgade 3 ❶ 86 13 06 44
Ⓦ www.cafeenglen.dk ⏱ 10.00–24.00 Mon–Sat, 11.00–24.00 Sun

Il Mercantino £–££ ❹ A delightful Italian restaurant and deli
selling fantastic sandwiches. ❹ Mejlgade 18 ❶ 86 12 00 48
Ⓦ www.il-mercantino.dk ⏱ 16.00–22.00 Tues–Sun, closed Mon

🔺 *Pasta galore at Il Mercantino*

AFTER DARK

RESTAURANTS

Teater Bodega ££ ⑤ Lively restaurant and bar frequented
by actors and artists. Photographs and posters line the walls,
telling the history of Aarhus's theatre scene. ⓐ Skolegade 7
ⓣ 86 12 19 17 ⓦ www.teaterbodega.dk ⓒ from 11.30 Mon–Sat,
Kitchen 11.30–22.30 Mon–Sat, closed Sun

Restaurant Mellemrum ££–£££ ⑥ A lovely restaurant located
away from the busier parts of the city centre that prides itself
on simple, modern dishes from the French kitchen. Limited

menu with only three starters, main courses and desserts, but service is excellent. ⓐ Fredens Torv 2 ⓣ 86 17 18 38 ⓦ www.restaurantmellemrum.dk ⓛ 17.00–23.00 Tues–Sat, closed Sun & Mon

BARS & CLUBS

Café Smagløs One of Aarhus's liveliest cafés and music venues, with a uniquely relaxed atmosphere. ⓐ Klostertorvet 7 ⓣ 86 13 51 33 ⓦ www.smagloes.dk ⓛ 09.30–24.00 Mon–Thur, 09.30–03.00 Fri & Sat, 09.30–12.00 Sun

Ris Ras Filliongongong Fantastic, relaxing local bar serving over 100 different beers. It does not serve food, but you are welcome to bring your own and eat it here, smoke a water pipe or play a board game with friends. ⓐ Mejlegade 24 ⓣ 86 18 50 06 ⓦ www.risras.dk ⓛ 12.00–02.00 Mon–Sat, 16.00–24.00 Sun

Studenterhus An important student institution that's housed in Pakhuset by the harbour, and is open to the general public. Live music three times a week, nightly DJ and bar. ⓐ Nordhavnsgade 1 ⓣ 86 18 30 21 ⓦ www.studenterhusaarhus.dk ⓛ Check website for opening hours, Reception 14.00–16.00 Mon–Thur

Under Masken Another institute in Aarhus's pub/bar life popular with artists and actors. Worth a visit just to see the freaky masks and theatre memorabilia bringing the walls and ceilings alive. ⓐ Bispegade 4 ⓣ 86 18 22 66 ⓛ 12.00–02.00 Mon–Sat, 12.00–24.00 Sun

Trøjborg & the North

To the northern side of the city centre are many important cultural sights such as the Stenomuseet, the Naturhisorisk (Natural History) Museum, the University of Aarhus, several other academic institutes and the beautiful Vennelyst Parken (see page 85). To the north of these is the residential district of Trøjborg. Like Frederiksbjerg, Trøjborg has a life of its own that's quite separate from that of Aarhus. Being in such close vicinity to the higher education institutes makes this is a popular district among the students who consitute two-thirds of all the inhabitants in Trøjborg. Not surprisingly, the atmosphere here is decidedly laid back and relaxed. In 2000, Aarhus municipality, with support from the By- and Boligministeriet (Ministry for Towns and Housing), set aside an astounding 10 million kroner for the further development of housing and garden areas here and for making improvements to the infrastructure and cultural and community life of Trøjborg. So, over the next decade or so, watch this space.

SIGHTS & ATTRACTIONS

Danmarks Japanske Have (Denmark's Japanese Garden)

A 20-minute bus journey north of Aarhus takes you to one of Denmark's most distinctive and prestigious international attractions. This highly original concept brings together all of the attributes Japanese culture is most famed for (except for sushi). Once within the gates you can take a peaceful walk around the beautiful Zen Garden. With a multitude of different

⬥ *Denmark's Japanese Garden*

Den Permanente

SALONVEJEN

❻

Riis Skov

VITUS BERINGS ROAD
HANS EGEDES VEJ
ROALD AMUNDSENS VEJ
SKOVFALDET
BA SALINS GADE

LAUGE KOCHS VEJ
FRIDTJOF NANSENS VEJ

KNUD RASMUSSENS VEJ
MYLIUS ERICHSENS VEJ

SKOVVANGSVEJ

NORDRE RINGGADE

SKOVVANGSVEJ

MARIENLUNDS ALLÉ
RUGBAKKEVEJ

❶ ❺
PEDER SKRAMS GADE

STEEN BILLES TORV
STEEN BILLES GADE

CORT ADELERS GADE

HERLUF TROLLES GADE

MARIENLUNDSVEJ

WILLEMOESGADE

OTTO RUDS GADE
TORDENSKJOLDSGADE

TRØJBORG

DRONNING MARGRETHES VEJ

❹
NIELS JUELS GADE

❷ OVE GJEDDES GADE

TRØJBORGVEJ

Nordre Kirkegård

KIRKEGÅRDSVEJ

SKOVVEJEN

ØST BOULEVARDEN

❸

🚆 Østbanetorvet

SVERIGESGADE

▪	...........POI
✝	...........Cathedral
ℹ	...........Information
🅟	..Police Station
✈	...........Airport
🚆	.....Railway Stn
🚌	......Bus Station
✚	...........Hospital

Trøjborg & the North

0 _____ 250 metres
0 _____ 250 yards

types of flowers and trees, including bamboo and bonsai, the scents and sights here can be savoured all year round. If you are partial to Japanese design, check out Zen Room. This design store is paradise for those looking for that unique something extra for the interior or exterior of the home. You'll find designer furnishings, garden furniture, pieces of art and various textiles, all produced with environmental awareness in mind and all free of artificial products. Zen Bath Wellness Centre is the place to go to find that sometimes elusive inner peace. Take an aromatherapy spa bath, have a full-body massage or, if you feel adventurous, try the hot stone massage. There are plenty of different options and packages to choose from. Last, but far from least, you can give your taste buds a treat at Restaurant WH, named after one of Denmark's most celebrated chefs, Wassim Hallal. Strangely enough, this 6-star restaurant does not serve Japanese food, but rather takes advantage of the high-quality Danish produce that can be found in this part of Jutland. ⓐ Randersvej 395, Trige ⓣ 72 20 08 87 ⓦ www.danmarksjapanskehave.dk ⓝ Regional bus 117 from the central bus station to Trige, Randersvej/Østermøllevej

DEN PERMANENTE

On the beach side of Riis Skov you will find this old-fashioned public bathing area. There are shower facilities and, down at the beach, there are some separate bathing areas for men and women; this stretch is famous for its nature-loving nude bathers. ⓐ Strandvej 2, Riis Skov ⓝ Bus: 1, 6, 8, 16, 56, 58

Riis Skov (Riis Forest)

In the 1800s this forest became the private property of the monarchy. This meant that Århusianers could only use it for pleasure – they were forbidden to work on it. To this day the forest's main function is that of recreation, with two hiking routes mapped out, a wonderful youth hostel, a playground for the kids, and the bathing area down by the bay and the wonderful restaurant Sjette Frederiks Kro (see page 89). The forest has mainly birch and oak trees, many of which are over 150 years old. Ash and maple trees can also be found. There are four stones/rocks of great importance in the forest: one is from a meteorite that exploded over Denmark in 1951, and the other three are memorials to Queen Margrethe. ⓐ Dronning Magrethes Vej/Grenåvej Ⓝ Bus: 6, 9, 16 to Riis Skov

Skt Johannes Kirke & Nordre Kirkegård

The church in Aarhus is no different from any of the other institutes in the city: Skt Johannes Kirke actively joins in the city's cultural events such as Århus Festuge and the Jazz Festival, and encourages members of the parish to participate in events by giving them a little twist. It welcomes students to discuss films with religious and ethical content; it holds a 'Service and Spaghetti' evening on the first Tuesday of the month from May to the end of September and an 'Open House' every Thursday between 14.00–16.30.

The nearby cemetery, Nordre Kirkegård (Northern Cemetery), is one of the most used green areas in the city of Aarhus. It dates back to 1876 and was originally opened due the lack of space in Søndre Kirkegård (Southern Cemetery) in the south of Aarhus.

83

The University of Aarhus, renowned for its greenery

This plot put the 'No Vacancies' sign up after just 42 years, and so came Vestre Kirkegård (Western Cemetery) to the west of the city. With numerous rare varieties of flora and fauna, the Nordre Kirkegård has a park-like feel and is often used as a place of rest for the living Århusianers. Look out for the exquisite statues and monuments dotted around the place. ⓐ Kirkegårdsvej 26 ⓣ 89 40 27 65 ⓦ www.aarhuskommune.dk ⓝ Bus: 1 to Kirkegårdsvej

Universitetsparken (University Park)

Just behind Vennelyst Parken and opposite Århus Sygehus (Aarhus Hospital) is University Park, home to **Århus Universitet** (the University of Aarhus ⓐ Norde Ringgade 1 ⓣ 89 42 11 11 ⓦ www.au.dk), Stenomuseet (Steno Museum, see page 86), the Statsbibliotek (the state library) and the Naturhistorisk Museum (the Natural History Museum, see page 86). With its two lakes, this area is another fabulous place to stop for a break, though it's a little busier than some of the other chill-out zones as it is the heart of the university. ⓐ Nørrebrogade ⓝ Bus: 3, 11, 56, 58, 90 to Nørrebrogade

Vennelyst Parken (Vennelyst Park)

A delightful park that used to be the grounds of the Århus Kunstmuseum. At present the Syplejehøjskole (The Danish Nursing School) has its HQ here. The park itself is a great place to take your sandwich and relax during a busy sightseeing day, and is popular with bird- and nature-watchers. The park hosts the Århus Middelalderfestival (see page 13) at midsummer and other cultural events during the year. ⓐ Høegh-Guldbergs Gade ⓝ Bus: 3, 11, 56, 58, 90 to Nørrebrogade

CULTURE

Naturhisorisk Museum (Natural History Museum)

The Natural History Museum's exhibits reflect the bent of its research department, and that is concentrated on entomology, fresh-water ecology, the eco-system, fauna and bioacoustics. It's a good idea to check the website to find out what the exhibition is at the time of your visit. ⓐ Wilhem Meyers Allé 210 ⓣ 86 12 97 77 ⓦ www.naturhistoriskmuseum.dk ⓛ 10.00–16.00 Mon–Fri, Sept–May; 10.00–17.00 Mon–Fri, Jul & Aug, closed Sat & Sun Ⓝ Bus: 3, 11, 56, 58, 90 to Nørrebrogade. Admission charge, under 18s free

Stenomuseet (Steno Museum – History of Science & Medicine)

There are four sections to this undeniably fab museum. The History of Science is split in two, with a chronological exhibition stretching from the prehistoric times to the end of the 1600s in which old telescopes, thermometers, barometers and apparatus make attractive exhibits. The other thematic exhibition covers astronomy and time, landscaping, optics, electromagnetism, nuclear physics, radio, arithmetic and chemistry. The History of Medicine's first floor has a chronological exhibition, which starts with an Egyptian mummy and an overview of Egyptian medical procedures from as far back as 1000 BC. On the ground floor there are a number of rooms reconstructed to depict an old dentist's surgery, a hospital laboratory and an operating room. There is also a small planetarium and a lovely Urtehaven (herb garden), with over 400 different herb species. ⓐ C F Møllers Allé, Bldg.100, Universitetsparken ⓣ 89 42 39 75 ⓦ www.stenomuseet.dk

🕐 09.00–16.00 Tues–Fri, 11.00–16.00 Sat & Sun, closed Mon
Ⓝ Bus: 3, 11, 56, 58, 90 to Nørrebrogade. Admission charge,
under 18s free

RETAIL THERAPY

Tordenskjoldsgade is the principal street in Trøjborg for
shopping, though the main reason for being in this street
is really the cafés. For gifts, souvenirs, clothes and bits and
bobs for the home it is best to head back into town through
the cemetery (delicately, there) along Mejlegade to the Latin
Quarter and Strøget.

Paustian Located in the station house, Østbanegård, by the
harbour (that's what you call a Paustian fact), this renowned
designer furniture house is well worth a browse for inspiration,
even if the pieces are a tidge beyond your budget. ⓐ Skovvejen 2
🕐 86 20 89 89 Ⓦ www.paustian.dk 🕐 09.30–17.30 Mon–Thur,
09.30–18.00 Fri, 10.00–15.00 Sat, closed Sun Ⓝ Bus: 6, 7, 9, 16
to Østbanetorvet; train to Østbanegård

TAKING A BREAK

There are numerous cafés along Tordenskjoldsgade (Ⓝ Bus: 1
to Niels Juuls Gade). If you fancy a picnic in one of the parks or
even the forest, try the baker's, **Bavinchi** (ⓐ Tordenskjoldsgade 18
🕐 86 16 84 43), and for cold cuts or some *smørrebrød*, look no
further than the butcher, **Kød Hjørnet** (ⓐ Tordenskjoldsgade 66
🕐 86 16 80 87).

Dolce Vita £ ❶ A fantastic ice cream and coffee shop that serves some imaginative coffee/ice cream combinations. ⓐ Tordenskjoldsgade 81 ❶ 86 10 38 30 Ⓦ www.dolcevita-aarhus.dk ◐ 12.00–22.00

Rohdes £ ❷ Very popular snack bar serving sandwiches, bagels and crêpes: eat in or take away. ⓐ Tordenskjoldsgade 22 ❶ 86 16 93 95 Ⓦ www.caferohdes.dk ◐ 10.00–21.00

🔻 *Join the locals for a drink in the cafés on Tordenskjoldsgade*

Fredes Flyvende Tallerken £–££ ❸ A nice, bright café,
sandwich bar and take-away by the harbour that's justly
famous for its chunky chips. ⓐ Østbanetorvet 2 ⓣ 61 60 92 57
ⓦ www.fredesflyvendetallerken.dk ⓛ 11.00–21.00 Mon–Sat,
12.00–21.00 Sun ⓝ Bus: 6, 7, 9, 16 to Østbanetorvet; train to
Østbanegård

AFTER DARK

Chez Toni £ ❹ Fantastic little family-run restaurant offering
reasonably priced Greek home cooking. ⓐ Tordenskjoldsgade 25
ⓣ 86 16 88 30 ⓦ www.cheztony.dk ⓛ 15.00–23.00 Mon–Fri,
closed Sat & Sun

Café Ziggy ££ ❺ Small, cosy restaurant and café serving
delicious snacks and sandwiches. ⓐ Tordenskjoldsgade 96
ⓣ 86 10 43 22 ⓦ www.cafeziggy.dk ⓛ 10.00–24.00 Mon & Tues,
10.00–01.00 Wed–Sat, 10.00–24.00 Sun, Kitchen 10.00–21.30

Sjette Frederiks Kro £££ ❻ It is well worth the trek to dine
in this great restaurant, serving wholesome French country
dishes. In wintertime it's a nice place to drink a cup of hot
chocolate after a long walk in the forest. ⓐ Salonvejen 1, Risskov
ⓣ 86 16 14 00 ⓦ www.sjettefrederikskro.dk ⓛ from 11.00 Tues
& Wed according to reservations ⓝ Bus: 6, 9, 16 to Riis Skov
ⓘ Reservation is a must

Frederiksbjerg & the South

The area directly south of the train station is known as
Frederiksbjerg. Those who live in this district do not really
need to go into Århus Midtby unless it is for a special occasion,
but of course as a visitor, you'll want to zip about all over the
place. M P Bruuns Gade and Frederiks Allé are the two main
streets; the former is rather more chic and trendy, with lovely
cafés, delis, a gourmet greengrocer's, Kong Gulerod (King Carrot!),
and boutiques. Frederiks Allé is perhaps a touch more downmarket,
with lots of *bodegas*, second-hand book shops, supermarkets and
fast-food places. Connecting these two streets is the popular
Jægergårdsgade (Ⓝ Bus: 4, 18, 24 to Jægergårdsgade), which
is a hang-out for Aarhus's 25- to 30-somethings. On the stretch
between M P Bruuns Gade and Frederiks Allé, you will find
a couple of Aarhus's best restaurants, several interior design
shops, a few *værtshuser*, a great pizza place and some handy
supermarkets. There is even an environmentally friendly
hairdresser, **Birthe Gleerup** (ⓐ Jægergårdsgade 63 ① 86 12 20 03
ⓦ www.birthe-gleerup.dk). Don't miss the fruit and veg market
on Ingerslev Boulevard on Wednesdays and Saturdays near
St Paul's Church.

SIGHTS & ATTRACTIONS

Marselisborg Havn (Marselisborg Harbour)
Marselisborg Harbour, developed during the early 1980s,
is the main harbour for pleasure boats. Located just south of the
somewhat less than attractive Multiterminal, there is space for

Roses in full bloom in front of the beautiful Marselisborg Palace

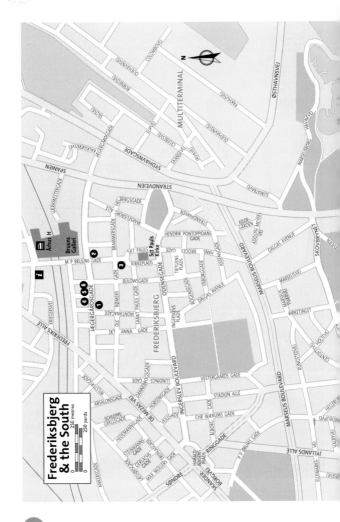

Frederiksbjerg
& the South

0   250 metres
0   250 yards

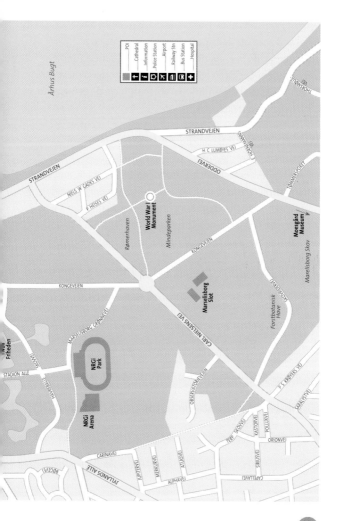

POI
Cathedral
Information
Police Station
Airport
Railway Stn
Bus Station
Hospital

Århus Bugt

STRANDVEJEN

H C LUMBYES VEJ

ODDERVEJ

STRANDVEJEN

NIELS W GADES VEJ

A HEISES VEJ

Rømerhaven

World War I Monument

Mindeparken

KONGEVEJEN

Moesgård Museum

Marselisborg Skov

KONGEVEJEN

Marselisborg Slot

Fortbotanisk Have

MARSELISBORG CYKELSTI

CARL NIELSENS VEJ

SKOVBRYNET

P S KRØJERS VEJ

Tivoli Friheden

NRGI Park

OBSERVATORIEVEJEN

SKRÆNTVEJEN

STADION ALLÉ

HAVREVEJ

NRGI Arena

SØBAKKEN

TERP SKOVVEJ

KASTORVEJ

SIRIUSVEJ

POLLUXVEJ

ORIONVEJ

CARINAVEJ

JUPITERVEJ

MERKURVEJ

ATLASVEJ

ALPHAVEJ

CAPELLAVEJ

JYLLANDS ALLÉ

BØGEVEJ

up to 450 vessels here. This is the place to enjoy a beer or a tasty meal and soak up that special atmosphere found at sailing clubs the world over. As this is Aarhus, things are extremely informal, laid-back and relaxed. 📍 Marselisborg Havnevej 38 ☎ 86 19 86 44 🌐 www.mh@marselisborghavn.dk Ⓝ Bus: 6 to Chr. Flintenborgs Plads

Marselisborg Slot (Marselisborg Palace)

Unfortunately, this beautiful palace, currently used as the Queen's summer residence, is not open to the public; but the grounds are. The building, constructed between 1899 and 1902 and designed by the Danish architect Hack Kampmann, was a gift to the Crown Prince Christian X and Princess Alexandrine, who at that time also used the palace as a summer residence.

NRGI PARK

Take note, sports fans, for this is the sporting centre of Aarhus. With a capacity for 20,000 spectators, it is home to, among others, the city's scandalously under-achieving football club, AGF (Aarhus Gymnastik Forening – try making a terrace chant out of that). NRGi Park and its arena is also a popular venue for many different spectator sporting events, cultural events and big concerts (George Michael, Elton John and Depeche Mode have played here in recent years). 📍 Marselisborg Park, Stadion Allé 70 ☎ 89 38 60 00 🌐 www.atletion.dk Ⓝ Bus: 18, 19 to Århus Stadion

The park surrounding the palace was designed with an English garden in mind, hence the big lawns surrounded by trees. There is also a rose garden and herb garden, as well as some small statues and monuments. Marselisborg Skov, just south of the palace, is one of the older forests and it marks the beginning of a large forested area and deer park. The leafy forests in Aarhus are dominated by birch trees, almost a fifth of which are over 150 years old. The palace and surrounding gardens, parks and forest should not be missed if you are to fully appreciate the diversity of this wonderful city. ⓐ Kongevejen ⓦ www.kongehuset.dk Ⓝ Bus: 1, 19 to Mindeparken

Mindeparken (Memorial Park)

A tranquil memorial park that commemorates the Danes who lost their lives in World War I, Mindeparken was inaugurated by King Christian X in 1925. Located to the south of Frederiksbjerg, next to Marselisborg Slot (see page 94), the park covers an area of 12 ha (30 acres). The monument, positioned right in the middle, consists of a circular limestone wall on which are carved war scenes alongside a list of the names of 4,140 deceased Danish soldiers. Also in the park is the Forstbotanisk Have, a large botanical garden housing over 900 different tree and bush types from all over the world. Look out for the two small buildings known as the Donbækhusene. These have seen a bit of life in their time, having been homes to the servants of Marselisborg, homes to the forest workers and a storage facility for gardening equipment. Be sure to visit the beautiful Rømerhaven (Roman gardens) as well. Ⓝ Bus: 1, 19 to Mindeparken

Moesgård Museum

Just south of Marselisborg, along the coast, you will come to
Moesgård beach and the woods that envelop Moesgård Manor,
home to the archaeological and ethnographical Moesgård
Museum. This wonderful, family-friendly museum contains
ancient artefacts dating back to the Iron Age, many of which
were found in the nearby Illerup river valley. Its most famous
resident is the Grauballe man, the only completely preserved
bog-man in the world. The site also contains several reconstructed
Viking age houses, and there is a prehistoric pathway which takes
you through a reconstructed Iron Age house. There are also Stone
Age and Bronze Age graves and cult sites. ⓐ Moesgård Allé 20,
Højbjerg ⓣ 89 42 11 00 ⓦ www.moesmus.dk ⓛ 10.00–17.00
Apr–Sept; 10.00–16.00 Tues–Sun, closed Mon, Oct–Mar ⓝ Bus: 6
to Moesgård Museum. Admission charge, under 18s free

🔺 *Moesgård Manor, home to a fascinating museum*

Sct Pauls Kirke (St Paul's Church)

Built in 1880, the architecture of St Paul's church, like the Domkirke, was inspired by Byzantine form. Heavy dark wood furnishing beautifully offsets the pretty, white interior and simple (yet decorative) ceilings. A wonderful peculiarity of this church is its altarpiece, whose frame was made by a young woman who was still just an apprentice. The original crucifix, with a slender Christ sculpted from ivory, was stolen and then replaced in the 1960s. Every detail here tells a fascinating story, and the church combines 19th- and 20th-century architecture and design quite brilliantly. ⓐ Sct Pauls Kirkeplads ① 86 12 21 54 ⓦ www.sctpauls.dk

Tivoli Friheden (Tivoli Amusement Park)

The city's only amusement park now has rides and attractions for adults, alongside treats for the whole family to enjoy together and plenty for the kids alone. It started its days in 1903 as a restaurant by the name of Friheden, and throughout the century developed gradually, being alternately used as a concert venue, a cultural meeting spot, a mini golf course and, eventually, an amusement park. It's a park and it's amusing; you'd have thought its vocation would have been obvious. ⓐ Skovbrynet ① 86 14 73 00 ⓦ www.friheden.dk ① hours vary greatly, see website for details ⓝ Bus: 4, 24, 18 to Friheden

RETAIL THERAPY

Frederiksbjerg has three main destinations that will attract shoppers: Jægergårdsgade is great for locally produced ceramics,

interior design shops and music outlets; M P Bruuns Gade
(🅝 Bus: 4, 18, 24 to Jægergårdsgade) has some lovely food shops
and kids' clothes shops; and Bruuns Galleri (shopping centre)
for the usual high street shopping (clothes, sportswear,
mainstream art, etc).

A Mano Known for their high-quality Moroccan leather cushions
produced in Marrakech, this warm, atmospheric shop is a pleasure
to browse and get inspiration for your home. 🅐 Jægergårdsgade 53
🅣 86 12 31 50 🅦 www.amano.dk 🅛 10.00–18.00 Mon–Sat

Made In A wonderful children's clothing and toy store. Also stocks
household items and decorative ornaments. 🅐 M P Bruuns Gade 35

🔻 *Almost everything for the kids in Made In...*

☎ 86 18 36 00 **🌐** www.madeinshop.dk **🕐** 10.00–17.30 Mon–Thur, 10.00–18.00 Fri, 10.00–15.00 Sat

Marianne Røgild Quaint ceramics workshop and retail outlet, selling sturdy, Danish-style earthenware. **ⓐ** Jægergårdsgade 55 **☎** 86761576 **🌐** www.kunstruten.dk **🕐** 12.00–17.30 Mon, 10.00–17.30 Tues–Fri, 10.00–13.00 Sat

TAKING A BREAK

There are numerous delightful cafés on Jægergårdsgade and M P Bruuns Gade as well as a couple of eateries in Bruuns Galleri.

D's Sandwich & Pizza £ ❶ Delicious and extremely popular pizzas and sandwiches with a Mediterranean twist. You can eat in or take away, and things get very busy at lunch time. **ⓐ** Jægergårdsgade 54 **☎** 73 72 00 00 **🌐** www.dsandwich.dk **🕐** 10.00–22.00 Mon–Sat, 12.00–22.00 Sun

Mademoiselle £ ❷ Toothsome sandwiches made with home-made bread and fresh local ingredients. Organic smoothies and juices. An extremely cosy little place. **ⓐ** M P Bruuns Gade 33 **☎** 86 12 20 53 **🌐** www.mademoiselle.dk **🕐** 11.00–19.00 Mon–Fri, 11.00–15.00 Sat, closed Sun

Schweizer Bageriet £ ❸ A delightful little bakery selling delectable cakes, biscuits and beverages. **ⓐ** M P Bruuns Gade 56 **☎** 86 12 34 47 **🌐** www.schweizerbageriet.dk **🕐** 06.30–18.00 Mon–Thur, 06.30–19.00 Fri, 06.30–17.00 Sat & Sun

AFTER DARK

RESTAURANTS

Klassisk 65 ££ ❹ Small wine bar and bistro serving high-quality, uncomplicated, good food in a totally relaxed atmosphere with great, friendly service. Fantastic wine and cheese selection. ⓐ Jægersgårdsgade 65 ❶ 86 13 12 21 ⓦ www.klassiskbistro.dk ⓛ 11.00–late Mon–Sat, 18.00–22.00 Sun

Rarbar ££ ❺ A cosy café, restaurant and bar that serves great cocktails, good food and also has a DJ playing three nights a week. Check out the SupperClub on Saturday nights: a three-course meal, prepared by the city's trainee chefs, and a cocktail cost 150kr. ⓐ Jægersgårdsgade 71 ❶ 86 19 60 80 ⓦ www.rarbar.dk ⓛ 11.00–01.00 Mon–Sat, 11.00–18.00 Sun

Malling & Schmidt £££ ❻ One of Aarhus's best fine-dining restaurants, with award-winning chefs and the finest quality raw ingredients. ⓐ Jægersgårdsgade 81 ❶ 86 17 70 88 ⓦ www.mallingschmidt.dk ⓛ 18.00–24.00 Tues–Sat, closed Sun & Mon

VÆRSTHUSER (PUBS)

Some of Aarhus's oldest pubs are located in Frederiksbjerg. If you happen to be in Jægergårdsgade pop in to **Pub'en**, which has been there since 1972 (ⓐ Jægergårdsgade 62 ❶ 86 13 60 98) and the lively **Jægerhytten** (ⓐ Jægergårdsgade 61 ❶ 86 12 22 75).

⊙ *The Sletterhage lighthouse has prime position at the seaside*

The Djursland Coastline: Aarhus to Ebeltoft

Aarhus lies on the southwestern border of the Djursland region which is famous for its beaches and wonderful coastline, hilly countryside, forests and tourist attractions. The coastal route from Aarhus to Ebeltoft takes you through some lovely small towns and villages. Djursland is a popular destination for Danish tourists during the summer vacation and is covered with summer houses. At Rønde you can visit some of Denmark's most ancient ruins. Ebeltoft is probably the town which reflects the charm of the whole region most, with its cobbled streets and half-timbered houses and beaches.

GETTING THERE

The most enjoyable way to take this trip is by car. Just follow route 15 out of Aarhus (along Kystvejen and Skovvejen, past Riis Skov), and turn off at route 21 just after you pass Rønde. This road takes you to the heart of Ebeltoft on Strandvejen.

Alternatively you can take the regional bus or train. Buses 120, 121, 122 and 123 from the **Rutebilstation** (ⓐ Fredensgade ❶ 86 12 86 22 ⓦ www.midttrafik.dk) all stop in Følle and Rønde; there are frequent departures and the journey takes 45 minutes. From Aarhus to Ebeltoft take number 123; this departs every half hour between 08.30 and 16.30, and once an hour until 21.30.

For detailed maps and further information on Djursland contact the VisitAarhus Velkomstcenter located near the main

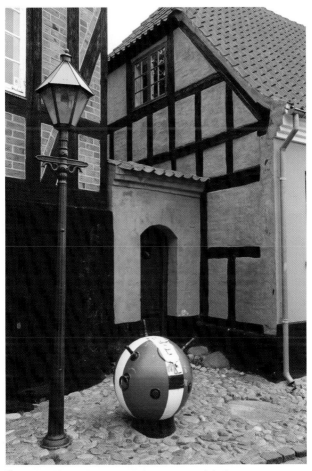

◓ *An unusual collection box, made from a mine at Ebeltoft*

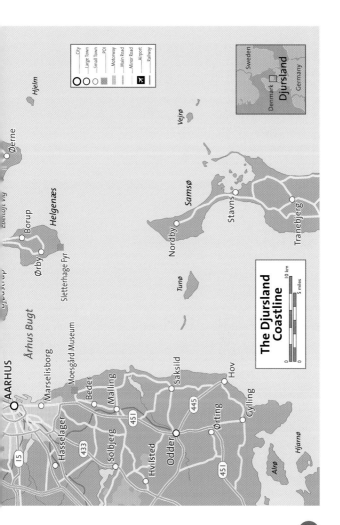

Hjelm

Øerne

Borup

Helgenæs

Ørby

Sletterhage Fyr

Ebeltoft Vig

Samsø

Vejrø

Stavns

Tranebjerg

Nordby

Tunø

Sweden

Denmark

Djursland

Germany

The Djursland Coastline

10 km

5 miles

AARHUS

Marselisborg

Moesgård Museum

Beder

Malling

Saksild

Hov

Solbjerg

451

Ørting

Gylling

Hvilsted

Odder

451

Hjarnø

Alrø

445

Hasselager

433

15

Århus Bugt

City
Large Town
Small Town
POI
Motorway
Main Road
Minor Road
Airport
Railway

> **IF YOU DO LIKE TO BE BESIDE THE SEASIDE…**
>
> … Djursland is the place for you. With the sea on almost three-quarters of its borders, every beach here is a winner, especially Grenå Strand, Ebeltoft Strand, Følle Strand at Kalø and Femmøller Strand. And it's not just about setting up your deckchair and wearing your handkerchief as a hat – the coves at Ebeltoft and Kalø are particularly popular with surfers and divers and are surrounded by beautiful scenery.

train station (see page 137). Otherwise contact **VisitDjursland** (📞 87 52 18 00 🌐 www.visitdjursland.com).

SIGHTS & ATTRACTIONS

Ebeltoft

Ebeltoft is officially the cleanest town in Denmark. In July and August you have the opportunity to join a free guided tour of this quaint little place, every Tuesday at 18.30 starting at Grisetorvet, or you could simply follow the night watchmen every evening as they take different routes keeping an eye on what's going on in the town. Adelgade is the main shopping street and is littered with 18th-century half-timbered buildings that uphold the spirit and simplicity of the Old Town.

The famous **Fregatten Jylland** (ⓐ Fregatøen 📞 86 34 10 99 🌐 www.fregatten-jylland.dk 🕐 10.00–16.00 Jan–Mar, Nov & Dec; 10.00–17.00 Apr–June, Sept & Oct; 10.00–19.00 July & Aug), the

🔺 *The wooden warship Fregatten Jylland is moored at Ebeltoft*

so-called ship that would not die, is moored here. It is the longest wooden ship in the world, and after sailing as a war vessel, became the royal ship for several years. This is a fantastic place for children and there are special events throughout the year.

Ebeltoft Zoo and Safari Park, **Ree Park** (ⓐ Stubbe Søvej 15 ❶ 86 33 61 50 Ⓦ www.reepark.dk ❿ 10.00–17.00 May & June & mid-Aug–Sept; 10.00–19.00 Jul–mid-Aug), is another favourite with children. As is **Jump'n'Fun** (ⓐ Erhvervsparken 2–4 ❶ 89 53 14 41 Ⓦ www.jumpnfun.dk), an indoor activity centre with climbing wall, table tennis, table football, board games, a pirate ship and loads more.

Ebeltoft has many fun cultural events throughout the year. In mid-October there is the **Ebelfestival** (❶ 86 34 38 55 Ⓦ www.ebelfestival.dk), which allows visitors to taste, smell, look at and feel all sorts of different apples in many different forms.

When it comes to grapes, the people of Ebeltoft stick to the wine form and hold an annual wine festival, **Vinfestival** (ⓐ Ndr Strandvej 3 ❶ 86 34 33 00 Ⓦ www.ebeltoft-vinfestival.dk), on the first weekend in March. Wines from Europe, South America, Africa, USA, Australia and New Zealand are on offer at Hotel Ebeltoft Strand, as well as in other restaurants and venues throughout the town.

The **Folkefestival** (ⓐ Fregatøen ❶ 22 62 64 31 Ⓦ www.folkefestival.dk), held over three days on Ascension Day weekend in May, is one of Ebeltoft's annual music events. Popular Danish folk and jazz bands get together and perform live at the superb Fregatten Jylland. **Ebeltoft Open Air** (Ⓦ www.ebeltoftopenair.dk) is another, and this is held at the end of July on the beach.

There are two museums any visit to Ebeltoft should include. **Det Gamle Rådhus (The Old Town Hall** ⓐ Juulsbakke 1 ⓘ 86 34 55 99 ⓦ www.ebeltoftmuseum.dk ⓛ 11.00–15.00 Sat & Sun, Dec–Apr; 11.00–15.00, May–mid-June & Sept; 11.00–17.00, mid-June–Aug), built in 1789 on the sight of the original town hall, houses part of Ebeltoft Museum. The main aim of the museum is to preserve the cultural artefacts that the town and neighbouring Rønde municipalities have inherited.

The stunning **Glasmuseet (Glass Museum** ⓐ Strandvejen 8 ⓘ 86 34 17 99 ⓦ www.glasmuseet.dk ⓛ 10.00–16.00 Nov–Mar; 10.00–17.00 Apr–June, Sept & Oct; 10.00–19.00 Jul & Aug), in the old Customs and Excise building, opened an amazing new wing in 2006. This new space has made room for a lovely café with views over the harbour, a bright exhibition space, a shop, reception and a glass-blowing studio where you can watch the artists at

▲ *The modern lines of the harbourside Glasmuseet*

work. The museum is home to a diverse collection of contemporary glass from all corners of the world; this is probably not a place to bring young children. In addition to the Glasmuseet, you will find several shops in town selling glassware, where the glassblowers are more than happy to show off their skills.

To find out more about what's on in Ebeltoft contact tourist information **Ebeltoft Mols Turistinformation** located near Fregatten Jylland (see map on pages 104–5) ⓐ S A Jensens Vej ① 86 34 14 00 ⓔ mail@ebeltoftby.dk

Helgenæs

Nowadays Djursland's southernmost point is largely uninhabited – the main reason for stopping here is to enjoy the views across the water to the neighbouring island of Samsø and to see Aarhus across the bay. There are two main look-out spots. The first, down by the water, is the Sletterhage Fyr (Sletterhage Lighthouse), which dates back to 1872. The other look-out tower, at a higher elevation, is the Tyskertårn (German Tower), which was built by the Germans during World War II. ⊗ Local bus: 361 from Rønde to Ørby

Mols Bjerge

The area of Mols is famous for the Mols Bjerge (Mols Mountains). These hills are as close as Denmark gets to mountains. The combination of absolute tranquillity and pretty scenery, with meadows and grazing cows on one side and the bay on the other, is something special. ⊗ www.skovognatur.dk ⊗ Alight from the bus at Femmøller and take a local bus, or walk through Mols Bjerge

⊗ *Rolling fields reach down to the sea in the region of Mols*

Rønde

If you want to visit one of Denmark's most well-preserved medieval castle ruins, this old trading town located inland from the Kalø Vig inlet is the place to alight. Kalø Slotsruin (Kalø Castle Ruins) covers a large area with the main castle building on a piece of land jutting out into the sea. The land linking the island to the mainland is a medieval artificial construction, which is also amazingly well preserved. To get to Kalø Slotsruin turn down Kaløvej (towards Ebeltoft); stop at the big car park and walk down to the ruins. Toilets, shop and information are all available here.

● *Fishing boats moored at Kalø*

The woods in Kalø are of equally great historical importance. There are an astounding 100 or so ancient monuments dating from the Stone and Bronze Ages here.

Nowadays, the town of Rønde is dominated by more modern buildings, but still has a seaside village feel to it. If you don't have the energy to take a tour of the ruins and woods, then you can get a great view of it all from the recently renovated **Bregnet Kirke** (ⓐ Kirkebakken ❶ 86 37 27 09).

Rønde Turistbureau ⓐ Ceresvej 2 ❶ 86372366 Ⓦ www.visitdjursland.dk

TAKING A BREAK

The best place to stop for a bite to eat in this area is Ebeltoft.

Café Bageriet £ Come here for a tasty, original light lunch. ⓐ Adelgade 60 ❶ 86 34 10 71

Chokoladehuset £ If you fancy a sweet snack, make sure you pop into this bakery and *chocolaterie*. ⓐ Adelgade 19

Gryden £ Head to this cosy family-run restaurant for a traditional, inexpensive Danish lunch. ⓐ Adelgade 32 ❶ 86 34 13 00 Ⓦ www.gryden.dk ❷ 10.00–21.00 Mon–Sat, 11.00–21.00 Sun, mid-Aug–mid-June; 10.00–23.00 Mon–Sat, 11.00–23.00 Sun, mid-June–mid-Aug

Mols og Fanø Bolsjer £ A quaint little confectioner. ⓐ Nedergade 11 ❶ 86 34 66 55

AFTER DARK

Mellem Jyder ££ A delightful restaurant that maintains its historical ambience with its furnishings and produces high standard traditional Danish meals using the best local ingredients. ⓐ Juulsbakke 3, Ebeltoft ① 86 34 11 23 Ⓦ www.mellemjyder.dk ② 12.00–late

Restaurant Hyttefadet ££ A wonderful restaurant at Ebeltoft harbour with an amazingly extensive fish and meat menu. ⓐ Havnevej 11A ① 86 34 46 47 Ⓦ www.restaurant-hyttefadet.dk ② 12.00–late Wed–Sun, closed Mon & Tues

Restaurant Nils £££ Great for a gourmet dinner with good wines and excellent service. ⓐ Adelgade 62, Ebeltoft ① 86 34 44 66 ② 11.00–late Tues–Sat, closed Sun & Mon

ACCOMMODATION

Accommodation in this area is a little limited, so be sure to book in advance.

Danhostel Ebeltoft £ A cosy little youth hostel five minutes' walk from the centre of Ebeltoft and a short canter up from the beach. In the evenings you can snuggle up in front of the open fire or enjoy your meal in the pretty back yard. ⓐ Søndergade 43 ① 86 34 20 53 Ⓦ www.danhostel.dk

Danhostel Rønde £ A great youth hostel lurks within this lovely, half-timbered house; there are parking facilities,

⬥ *A solitary old farmhouse at Kalø*

and you can hire a bike here. ⓐ Grenåvej 10B ⓣ 86 37 11 08
ⓦ www.danhostel.dk

Hotel Ebeltoft £–££ A basic, yet pleasant, hotel right in the heart
of Ebeltoft ⓐ Adelgade 44 ⓣ 86 34 10 90

Molskroen £££+ Spoil yourself with beautiful views, tranquillity,
good food, wine and warm hospitality. The restaurant was voted
Denmark's 2006 Restaurant of the Year. Perfect for a romantic
weekend away. ⓐ Hovedgaden 16, Femmøllerstrand
ⓣ 86 36 22 00 ⓦ www.molskroen.dk

The Djursland Coastline: cross country to Grenå

If you prefer to take in some inland adventures, there is plenty to see and do if you travel from east Djursland through some of the smaller towns and villages towards the seaside town of Grenå, the final stop on our coastal journey and Djursland's largest town. In this area you will also find three adjoining forests, Auning Skov, Fjeld Skov and Løvenholmskov.

◗ *The Kattegatcentret is one of the biggest attractions in the area*

GETTING THERE

From Aarhus, the 60-km (37-mile) journey to Grenå takes around 45 minutes, but the inland route will take you longer, depending on how many of the sights you decide to take in. Follow route 15 out of Aarhus (along Kystvejen and Skovvejen, past Riis Skov) to go straight to Grenå. If you want to see some inland sights, turn off heading east on route 587 just after you pass Løgten. At the first major right, head north on route 563. This will take you to the heart of Auning and on to route 16, which ends up by the sea at Grenå.

◔ One of the many rides at Djurs Sommerland

If you wish to take public transport, there are half-hourly trains from Århus H (see page 51) to Grenå.

SIGHTS AND ATTRACTIONS

Allingåbro

Just 30 minutes' drive north of Aarhus is the small town of Allingåbro. Fans of motor vehicles should visit in May when the one-day **Allingåbro Motor Festival** (ⓐ Hovedgaden 27, Allingåbro ⓣ 23 72 97 03 ⓦ www.motor-festival.dk ⓝ Regional bus: 119 from

> ### DJURS SOMMERLAND –
> ### DENMARK'S BIGGEST WATER PARK
> Heading east along route 16, this is a superb place in which to shiver one's timbers and amuse one's children. As well as the fantastic waterslide, the Colorado River ride and Cowboyland, there are lovely gardens to relax in. There is a large picnic area with barbecues where you can prepare your own food, and several eateries selling healthy sandwiches and salads as well as fast food. The theme of the park is becoming distinctly more piratical, which, of course, the little ones just love as it may ring certain bells in their minds. Idea for a film: Pirates of the Jutland Peninsula. ⓐ Randersvej 17 ⓣ 86 39 84 00 ⓦ www.djurssommerland.dk ⓛ irregular opening hours, see website for details ⓝ Regional bus: 121 from Århus Rutebilstation. Admission charge

Århus Rutebilstation) brings together motorbike, car, truck, moto cross, tractor (basically, anything with a motor) enthusiasts from around Denmark. Some of the events include drag racing, stock car racing, a classic car exhibition and a freight trucker exhibition.

Year round, **Djursland for fuld Damp (Full Steam Ahead in Djursland** ⓐ Hovedgaden 4, Allingåbro ⓣ 86 48 04 44 ⓦ www.dffd.dk ⓛ 09.00–17.00 May–Sept ⓝ Regional bus: 119 from Århus Rutebilstation) offers a variety of different activities including rental of a cycle-trolley. The tracks run through forests, fields and by the fjord with picnic areas to stop at along the way. There are also canoes to rent if you feel like a water adventure. In July and August, take a slow ride through the forest and along the fjord on an old steam train. You can also visit the small museum, hire an old bus for a sightseeing tour, or spend a few nights in an old sleeping car or in the old station warehouse, both of which have been converted to provide accommodation.

Auning Kart Park

Just to the south of Allingåbro is Auning. Denmark's best go-kart track, Auning Kart Park is located half-way between the two. There are good facilities and a café and big terrace with a great view over the track for spectators. ⓐ Dammelstrupvej 1 ⓣ 86 49 27 49 ⓦ www.auningkartpark.dk ⓛ 16.00–20.00 Wed & Thur, 12.00–20.00 Fri, 09.00–18.00 Sat, 12.00–18.00 Sun, Apr–June & Aug–Oct; 12.00–20.00 Tues–Thur, 12.00–18.00 Fri & Sun, 09.00–18.00 Sat, July; by appointment Nov–Mar ⓝ Regional bus: 119 from Århus Rutebilstation. Admission charge, under-18s free

Djurslands Jernbanemuseum (Djursland Railway Museum)

Just south of Djurs Sommerland in the town of Ryomgård, you'll find this tiny museum where you can visit the train depot which dates back to 1908, see the exhibition telling the history of Danish railways, take a look at some of the old steam train engines and carriages, or admire the wonderfully detailed model railways.
ⓐ Museumsvej 2 ⓘ 86 39 59 11 ⓦ www.djbm.dk ⓛ variable, so check website ⓝ Regional bus: 121 from Århus Rutebilstation; Århus H – Grenå train to Ryomgård. Admission charge

Grenå

Historically a market town, Grenå has several different types of specialist shops and supermarkets and a fairly busy harbour. Grenå Å (Grenå river) runs through the town centre, linking it to the harbour. At the heart of the town is Torvet (the Square) with the church at its centre. Just opposite the church you'll find the tourist information **Grenå Turistbureau** (ⓐ Torvet 1 ⓘ 87 58 12 00 ⓦ www.visitdjursland.dk). In 2006, the long, sandy, white Grenå Strand was voted Jutland's best beach, due to its child-friendliness, excellent facilities and extremely clean water.

Probably the most famous tourist attraction in Grenå is **Kattegatcentret (The Kattegat Centre** ⓐ Færgevej 4 ⓘ 86 32 52 00 ⓦ www.kattegatcentret.dk ⓛ times vary considerably during the year, check website or call for details). This amazing marine wildlife centre is one of a kind where both adults and children have the opportunity to get into closer contact with marine life. The centre has created a spacious environment for its inhabitants and visitors. The massive aquariums allow you to get a close view

● *View all the marine life while 'in the water' at the Kattegatcentret*

of hundreds of different types of marine life. There is daily feeding of the sharks, seals and the fish in the tropical lagoon, and you can do an introductory scuba dive in the same tanks as the sharks.

Skandinavisk Dyrepark (Scandinavian Wildlife Park)

Great for nature-lovers, this fantastic park in Kolind is set in authentic Scandinavian countryside and is home to over 300 animals. From brown bears to Landrace goats, moose and wolves, the animals have plenty of space to roam around in their natural environment. The Mammoth Activity Centre is the only place in Europe where you can see a full-sized mammoth skeleton.
ⓐ Nødagervej 67B ⓣ 86 39 13 33 ⓦ www.skandinaviskdyrepark.dk

🕐 10.00–17.00 May & June, mid-Aug & Sept; 10.00–18.00 July–mid-Aug; 10.00–16.00 Tues–Thur, 10.00–17.00 Sat & Sun, Sept–mid-Oct; 10.00–17.00 13 Oct–21 Oct 🚌 Regional bus: 120 from Århus Rutebilstation; Århus H – Grenå train to Kolind. Admission charge

CULTURE

Djurslands Museum & Dansk Fiskerimuseum (Danish Fishing Museum)

These are housed in the beautiful old half-timbered yellow building near the church on the main square of Grenå. Together, the museums have a curious collection of artefacts dating back to the year 1000. ⓐ Søndergade 1, Grenå ☎ 86 32 48 00 🌐 www.djurslandsmuseum.dk 🕐 10.00–16.00 Mon–Fri, 13.00–16.00 Sat & Sun, mid-June–Aug; 13.00–16.00 Tues–Fri & Sun, closed Sat, Sept–mid-June

Gammel Estrup & Dansk Landbrugmuseum

Close to the small town of Auning, you will find two wonderful places of historical interest. The first is Gammel Estrup, a museum housed in the beautiful Gammel Estrup Manor House, whose farm houses are home to the second attraction, Dansk Landbrugmuseum (The Danish Agricultural Museum).

Gammel Estrup is a beautiful Renaissance manor with a baroque garden and carp ponds. Through changing exhibitions and events visitors to the museum can learn about the life of Danish aristocracy (and their servants). As well as the permanent exhibition, there are activities happening all year round in which

staff dress in period costume. ⓐ Randersvej 2, Auning ⓣ 86 48 30 01
ⓦ www.gammelestrup.dk ⓛ 10.00–15.00 Tues–Sun, Nov–Mar;
10.00–17.00 Apr–June & mid-Aug–Oct; 10.00–18.00 July–mid-Aug

The Dansk Landbrugsmuseum is an agricultural museum.
Its huge collection of old vehicles and farming equipment brings
you close to some of the past wonders of the farming world.
The old smithy is housed in a building that dates back to 1761.
ⓐ Randersvej 4, Auning ⓣ 86 48 34 44 ⓦ www.gl-estrup.dk
ⓛ 10.00–15.00 Tues–Sun, Feb, Mar, Nov & Dec; 10.00–17.00,
Apr–June & mid-Aug–Oct; 10.00–18.00 Jun–mid-Aug

🔺 The Djurslands Museum & Dansk Fiskerimuseum in the centre of Grenå

RETAIL THERAPY

All of the aforementioned sights, attractions and cultural institutes have their own gift-shops where you can purchase souvenirs of your trip. If you are a pottery-lover you should visit **Pottehuset**, north of Nimtofte in Nørager, to find high-quality Danish pottery. ⓐ Keramikvej 6 ① 86 48 63 65 ⓦ www.pottehuset.net ① 10.00–17.00 Whitsun–mid-Sept

TAKING A BREAK

If the weather is fine, you really should take advantage of the marvellous countryside and bring along a picnic hamper. Alternatively, grab a bite to eat at the eateries found in the larger attractions listed. There are a few different places to try in the larger town, Grenå, but do not expect to find many food options in the smaller towns and villages.

AFTER DARK

There is not much to do in these locations after dark, so your best bet is to either head back to Aarhus or down to Ebeltoft (see page 114).

Helnan Marina Hotel ££ This hotel in Grenå has a lovely restaurant with an exciting, international menu that's designed according to what is in season. ⓐ Kystvej 32, Grenå ① 86 32 25 00 ① 18.00–22.00 Mon–Sat, closed Sun

● *The wild landscape of the coastline near Gjerrild*

ACCOMMODATION

For cheaper options, head to Danhostel Rønde or Ebeltoft
(see page 114). Otherwise in Grenå there are the Helnan Marina
Hotel (see page 125) or the nearby **Gjerrild Kro**, a wonderful
Danish inn with 19 rooms in two buildings that date back to 1843.
ⓐ Gjerrild Bygade 16 ⓣ 86 38 40 51 ⓦ www.gjerrild-kro.dk

● *Crossing the bridges over the canal in Aarhus*

PRACTICAL
information

Directory

GETTING THERE
By air

Ryanair is the only budget airline currently operating flights from London Stansted to Aarhus Airport (see page 50). In addition, from Aarhus airport Scandinavian Airlines operates scheduled flights to and from Copenhagen, British Airways to and from Oslo, and Finnair to and from Oslo. From Billund Lufthavn, which has a one-hour bus connection to Aarhus, there are scheduled flights to all the major cities in Europe, such as Amsterdam, Berlin, Prague, London, Gothenburg, Madrid, Milan, Munich and Dublin. In England there are connections to Billund via British Airways to and from Birmingham and Manchester, Sterling to and from London Gatwick and Ryanair to and from London Stansted.

British Airways ⓦ www.ba.com
Finnair ⓦ www.finnair.com
Ryanair ⓦ www.ryanair.com
Scandinavian Airlines (SAS) ⓦ www.sas.dk
Sterling ⓦ www.sterlingticket.com

Many people are aware that air travel emits CO_2, which contributes to climate change. You may be interested in the possibility of lessening the environmental impact of your flight through Climate Care, which offsets your CO_2 by funding environmental projects around the world. Visit ⓦ www.climatecare.org

By rail

This is probably the most expensive way to arrive in Aarhus unless you are travelling on an **Interrail**, **Eurorail** or **Scanrail** ticket (ⓦ www.scanrail.com). **Rail Europe** (ⓦ www.raileurope.co.uk) can book tickets on-line. A direct journey from the UK by rail will first involve a ferry journey from Harwich to Esbjerg in Jutland (see page 131) or the **Eurostar** to Brussels (ⓣ (UK) 08705 186186 ⓦ www.eurostar.com). Århus H is the main train station in the city (see page 51).

⬤ Yellow city buses and blue regional buses pass the Rådhus

By road

It is great to have a car if you are planning a longer stay as Aarhus is surrounded by beautiful countryside, and the rest of Jutlund offers numerous holidaying possibilities. Arriving from the UK, the least complicated route is to take the ferry from Harwich to Esbjerg (see opposite). From Zealand, take either one of the ferry options, or from Korsø drive across the Strobæltsbroen bridge and another of Denmark's islands, Fyn. Once you cross the bridge from Fyn to Jutland, you are about 75 minutes from Aarhus. If you are already on mainland Europe, the easiest route is through Germany via Hamburg (Jutland connects to Germany's northern border). For detailed road directions see ⓦ www.multimap.com

● *Aarhus's busy harbour*

Coach options are underwhelming. **Eurolines Scandinavia** offers a very limited service to Aarhus but does not have an office in the city (ⓘ 70 10 00 30 ⓦ www.eurolines.dk). There is a coach (number 888) that operates between Copenhagen and Aalborg, stopping in Aarhus at the main bus station, **Rutebilstation** ⓐ Fredensgade and Copenhagen Airport (and Valby S-train Station in the city – see ⓦ www.dsb.dk for further connections in Copenhagen). The journey takes around three hours, and there are five departures a day. ⓐ Graham Bellsvej 40 ⓘ 70 21 08 88 ⓦ www.abildskou.dk

By water

Coming from England you can take the ferry from Harwich to Esbjerg. **DFDS Seaways** has three scheduled departures per week all year round (ⓘ (UK) 0871 522 9955 (DK) 33 423 000 ⓦ www.dfds.co.uk). The trip from Esbjerg to Aarhus will take just under two hours by road or by train.

Travelling to and from Zealand, where Copenhagen is located, **Mols Linien** (ⓘ 70 10 14 18 ⓦ www.mols-linien.dk) operates two routes: Aarhus to Odden (45-minute boat trip; 90 minutes to Copenhagen) and Aarhus to Kalundborg (65-minute trip; 75 minutes to Copenhagen). There is no public transport from either port on Zealand, so a car is a must.

ENTRY FORMALITIES

If you have an EU, US, Canadian, Australian or New Zealand passport you do not need a visa; all other nationalities will require one. However, for stays longer than three months a residence permit is required. EU citizens can apply for this while in Denmark, but other nationals must obtain one before entering the country. Immigration control is very tight and you will be questioned about where you are staying, the purpose of your visit and how you intend to support yourself. EU residents may bring possessions and goods for personal use (including tobacco and alcohol) into Denmark, provided they have been bought in the EU. Residents of non-EU countries, and EU residents arriving from a non-EU country, are limited to a maximum of: 400 cigarettes and 50 cigars or 50 g (2 oz) tobacco; two litres (three bottles) of wine and one litre (approximately two pints) of spirits or liqueurs.

MONEY

The currency in Denmark is the Danish krone (kr) and the smaller units are øre (100øre = 1kr). Øre come in 25 and 50 øre pieces and are bronze in colour. The 1, 2 and 5kr pieces are silver in colour and ascend in size as with value. The 10 and 20kr pieces are golden colour, the 10kr being smaller in size than the 20kr. The main place to change money in Aarhus is at the banks which are located on the main streets in the city. Look out for Nordea, Jyske Bank, Spar Nord and Djurslands Bank. Banks do not keep large amounts of foreign currency, so make sure you change some at home. Forex bureau de change found on the main shopping street will have larger sums at hand ⓐ Ryesgade 28 ⓣ 86 80 03 40. Where there are banks, there are ATMs. Visa and MasterCard are accepted in most of the larger stores, but many of the smaller ones might not accept foreign (non-Danish) credit cards.

HEALTH, SAFETY & CRIME

No vaccinations or preventative medicines need to be taken before arriving in Denmark. The water is very clean and safe to drink from the tap. The Danish health care system is good. EU citizens need to have their European Health Insurance Card (EHIC) in order to claim any health care expenses upon return to their home country. A doctor's consultation will cost a minimum of 300kr. Travel insurance is essential to ensure you are covered in any case.

Aarhus is probably one of the safest cities in Northern Europe. The most trouble you may run into is when the nightclubs turn out in the early hours of the morning and there may be a few exuberant merry-makers roaming the streets around Vadestedet. Even so, do not take any unnecessary risks. If you do have anything stolen report it immediately to the police so that you can claim it on your insurance (see Emergencies, page 138, for numbers).

OPENING HOURS

Shops usually open at 09.30 or 10.00 and close 17.30 Monday to Thursday, 18.00–19.00 Friday and 14.00–15.00 Saturday. The bigger stores may have longer opening hours on Friday and Saturday. Shops are closed on Sundays. Many museums and attractions have late opening on Wednesdays (until 20.00–21.00) and are closed on Sundays. Some of the smaller ones also close on Mondays. Restaurants open at widely varying times, some from as early as 10.00, but most close their kitchen between 21.30 and 22.00. Banks are open 10.00–16.00 Monday to Friday and some open until 17.30 on Thursdays.

TOILETS

There are public toilets in the main train and bus station.
The department stores and some larger shops also have toilets.
Restaurants, bars and cafés don't usually mind if you ask to borrow
theirs. There are also several modern public toilets throughout
the city – they look like big, grey Tardises.

CHILDREN

Aarhus is very child friendly, as is the rest of Denmark. Entrance
to most of the museums is free for under-18s. Local buses and
all trains accommodate pushchairs and prams; public buildings
have lifts and ramps and people at hand to help. People offer
to help if they can see you need it.

Most of the museums and attractions have a children's
section. The junior museum in ARoS (see page 68) is a
particular favourite and
the Barndommens Museum
in the Kvindemuseet
(see page 71) is extremely
popular as it is a celebration
of childhood. As well
as Tivoli Friheden (see
page 97) there is **Legeland**
(ⓐ Holmstrupgårdvej 18,
Braband ❶ 86 24 11 22
ⓦ www.legelandet.dk
🕐 10.00–18.00 Wed–Sun,
closed Mon & Tues

○ Viking imagery on show at ARoS

🔵 Bus: 15 to Holmstrupgårdsvej. Admission charge), located just outside the city centre. This is a huge indoor playground with massive slides, bouncy castles and mini-golf. Just south of the city you will find Moesgård Museum (see page 96), an open-air museum with a forest and the beach as its boundaries, which is a great place to take children. This archaeological and ethnographical museum has numerous activities for children and is a fun, educational day out for the whole family.

COMMUNICATIONS
Internet
Internet cafés are non-existent in the city centre as everybody has access at home in Denmark. However, many cafés and public offices have free wireless access, as do the majority of hotels. The hostels, sleep-ins and several bed & breakfasts have internet access. You can use the computers in the library for free.

Phone
There are a few public telephones around, and they are either card or coin-operated. Phonecards come in denominations of 30, 50 and 100kr, and the coin-operated phones accept all coins from 1 to 20kr but do not give change.

If you are using your home mobile phone to call a Danish number, don't forget to precede the number with the country code for Denmark (45). So if you have an English phone then you would dial 0045 plus the eight-digit Danish number.

TELEPHONING DENMARK

The international dialling code for Denmark is 45. To dial any of the Danish numbers in this book from your own country, dial your own international access code (00 for the UK), then 45, then the eight-digit number. All private phones in Denmark have eight digits and there are no area codes.

TELEPHONING ABROAD

To dial abroad from Denmark, dial 00 followed by your own country's international code (UK 44, Ireland 353, USA and Canada 1, Australia 61, New Zealand 64, South Africa 27) and then the area code (leaving off the first 0) and number.

Post

Letters weighing up to 50 g to destinations within Denmark are 4.75kr. The same letter will cost 7.25kr to a European destination and 8.25kr to the rest of the world.

Main Post Office ⓐ Banegårdspladsen 1A ⓣ 80 20 70 30
ⓦ www.postdanmark.dk ⓛ 10.00–18.00 Mon–Fri,
10.00–13.00 Sat

ELECTRICITY

Denmark runs on 220V 50Hz AC and the Danish sockets are round two-pin ones. Adaptors are best bought in your home country, but you can find multi-pin adaptors in some electrical stores. Hotels will have square adaptors you can borrow.

TRAVELLERS WITH DISABILITIES

Aarhus is an extremely socially aware city, therefore you will find that almost all public areas, toilets and buildings, including shops and restaurants, are accessible to the disabled. Bus and train drivers are happy to help passengers embark and alight. For further information contact **Socialcenter Centrum**
ⓐ Valdemarsgade 18 ☏ 89 40 20 00

TOURIST INFORMATION

VisitAarhus Velkomstcenter is located near the main train station
ⓐ Banegårdspladsen 20 ☏ 87 13 50 10 ⓦ www.visitaarhus.com
🕑 Opening hours vary from year to year and season to season, so check website 🚍 Bus: all routes to Banegårdspladsen
Århus Rutebilstation (Århus rtb) is located next to the harbour
ⓐ Fredensgade ☏ 86 12 86 22 ⓦ www.bus-info.dk 🕑 07.00–22.00

BACKGROUND READING

Most of the books about Aarhus are only in Danish and have no English translation. However, the following will give you excellent background information on some of the key influences on the city:

Danish Chairs by Noritsugu Oda. This highly readable work provides explanation and context for the national obsession with design.

No Small Achievement: Special Operations Executive and the Danish Resistance, 1940–1945 by Knud JV Jespersen and Christopher Wade. A fascinating account of how the Danish psyche dealt with five years of occupation.

The Vikings by Else Roesdahl. The best of the many books about the horny-helmeted marauders who gave Aarhus its start in life.

Emergencies

For emergency fire, ambulance & police call 🛈 112 (toll-free)

MEDICAL SERVICES
Your hotel will have a list of doctors in the area. The fee must be paid in cash and will be a minimum of 300kr. Almost all doctors will speak excellent English.

Emergency medical professionals
Emergency doctor 🕓 16.00–08.00 Mon–Fri, 00.00–24.00 Sat & Sun 🛈 70 11 31 31
Emergency dentist 🛈 86 19 77 07
Emergency chiropractor 🛈 86 18 00 00
24-hour pharmacy – Løve Apotek 🅐 Store Torv 5 🛈 86 12 00 22

EMERGENCY PHRASES

Help! Can you help me?
Hjælp! Kan du hjæpe mig?
Yehlb! Ka do yehlbeh mai?

Call an ambulance/a doctor/the police!
Ring efter en ambulance/en læge/politiet!
Ring ehfda in ahmboolahnseh/in leh-eh/porlitee-eht!

Accident and Emergency – Århus Sygehus ⓐ Nørrebrogade 44
🛈 89 49 44 44 Ⓝ Bus: 14, 56, 58 to Århus Sygehus

POLICE

If you break down in your car call **Falck** 🛈 70 10 20 30
 Should you need to report a crime or a theft contact
Århus Police ⓐ Riddestræde 1 🛈 87 31 14 48 Ⓝ Bus: 3, 7, 14
to Rutebilstationen

EMBASSIES & CONSULATES

All embassies and consulates are located in Copenhagen.
You should contact the embassy if you need a replacement
passport. For matters involving the police, the embassy will
be unable to assist you.

Australian ⓐ Dampfærgevej 26 🛈 70 26 36 76
 ⓦ www.denmark.embassy.gov.au
British ⓐ Kastelsvej 36–40 🛈 77 34 86 51
 ⓦ www.britishembassy.dk
Canadian ⓐ Kristen Bernikowsgade 1 🛈 33 48 32 00
 ⓦ www.canada.dk
Irish ⓐ Østbanegade 21 🛈 35 42 32 33
South African ⓐ Gammel Vartov Vej 8 🛈 39 18 01 55
 ⓦ www.southafrica.dk
US ⓐ Dag Hammarskjölds Allé 24 🛈 35 41 71 00
 ⓦ www.usembassy.dk